PUGET SOUND

LAKE UNION

LAKE UNION

WASHINGTON'S FIRST WORLD'S FAIR

ALASKA·YUKON·PACIFIC EXPOSITION

A TIMELINE HISTORY

Alaska-Yukon-Pacific Exposition
Washington's First World's Fair
A Timeline History

By Alan J. Stein, Paula Becker & The HistoryLink.org Staff

Project director, Marie McCaffrey
Additional research, Jennifer Ott
Editors and proofreaders, Tom Brown and Priscilla Long
Design, Nancy Kinnear
Olmsted content consultants, Jerry Arbes and Anne Knight

Printed in China by C & C Offset Printing
Second printing: August 2009
A HistoryLink Book
Published by History Ink/HistoryLink in association with the
University of Washington Press

HistoryLink.org

www.historylink.org

ISBN 978-0-295-98926-6
Library of Congress Control Number: 2009921997

For more information on the Alaska-Yukon-Pacific Exposition,
go to www.historylink.org,
The Online Encyclopedia of Washington State History.
To find events, organizations, and conversations on the A-Y-P Exposition centennial
celebration, go to http://www.aype.org/, the A-Y-P Exposition Community.

Generous support for this book was provided by the Washington State Department
of Community, Trade & Economic Development, King County's 4Culture,
the City of Seattle's Mayor's Office of Arts & Cultural Affairs, and
a private donation by Chris Smith Towne.

seattle.gov   ayp100.org   www.cted.wa.gov

WASHINGTON'S FIRST WORLD'S FAIR

Alaska·Yukon·Pacific Exposition

A TIMELINE HISTORY

BY ALAN J. STEIN, PAULA BECKER & THE HISTORYLINK STAFF

In Memoriam
Walt Crowley (1947–2007)
Visionary, Historian, Founder of HistoryLink.org

CONTENTS

AUTHORIZED BIRDS EYE VIEW OF THE ALASKA-YUKON-PACIFIC EXPOSITION
SEATTLE, U.S.A. 1909
OPENS JUNE 1ST   CLOSES OCT. 16TH

FOREWORD

THE 1909 ALASKA-YUKON-PACIFIC EXPOSITION put Seattle on the national map when most of the country still considered the Pacific Northwest frontier country. The event showcased Seattle's transition from a village of dirt streets and wooden boardwalks to a bustling city of brick and steel, a growing metropolis poised to shape the region's destiny.

Only two decades earlier, Seattle's civic leaders dedicated themselves to rebuilding from the ashes of the Great Fire. In 1897, the arrival of two tons of gold from Alaska sparked even greater development. Tens of thousands of fortune seekers made their way to Washington, seeking transport north to the Klondike. Seattle was their gateway to riches, and eager treasure hunters bought most of their provisions here. Upon their return, some successful sourdoughs spread their wealth through bank investments and real estate ventures.

By 1907, Seattle had doubled in size, and civic leaders began planning a world's fair to showcase the region's new stature in the Pacific Northwest. Most crucially, the fair would highlight our ties to the Yukon and what we now call the Pacific Rim.

A century later, these connections still hold firm. After gold fever subsided, the economies of Seattle and Alaska grew in tandem from commercial fishing, the cruise ship industry, and the construction of the trans-Alaska oil pipeline right after the Boeing Bust of the 1970s (as with the gold rush, most workers and supplies for that project moved through Seattle, giving the city a big boost when it badly needed it).

In 2004, I called Walt Crowley, an old friend of mine and director of History Ink / HistoryLink.org (the online encyclopedia of Washington state history) and suggested that we think about ways to celebrate the Alaska-Yukon-Pacific Exposition centennial that was coming up in 2009. He suggested a number of new essays could be written for HistoryLink.org, and also a book, which you now hold in your hands. The book was, like the fair itself, the direct result of community effort. In 2005, the City of Seattle gathered together a centennial task force with Walt and Leonard Garfield, executive director of the Museum of History & Industry, as co-chairs. As a result of their efforts, and those of too many others to acknowledge here, the Alaska-Yukon-Pacific Exposition centennial will be celebrated throughout 2009 with scores of events throughout the state, and is commemorated in this volume.

Walt suffered an untimely death in 2007, and never got to see the completed book. I have no doubt he would have loved its vivid retelling of a cornerstone event in the city's history. So, I think, will you.

—Greg Nickels
Mayor of Seattle
February 1, 2009

INTRODUCTION

BY PAUL DORPAT

THE ALASKA-YUKON-PACIFIC EXPOSITION, Washington's first world's fair, took place on the University of Washington campus in Seattle between June 1 and October 16, 1909. More than three million visitors from around the state, the nation, and the world arrived to enjoy the fair. They viewed hundreds of agricultural, industrial, historical, and cultural exhibits, strolled the lushly manicured grounds, and were entertained by rides, games, and displays on the midway. Meanwhile Seattle promoted itself as a gateway to the rich resources of Alaska, the Yukon, and Asia.

The A-Y-P Exposition was first envisioned as a 10-year anniversary for the 1897 rush from the Seattle waterfront to gold on the Klondike River, accessed through Alaska. That Jamestown, Virginia, also claimed 1907 for its tercentenary celebration of the first permanent English settlement in North America gave our local A-Y-P enthusiasts a most fortunate break: They got two more years to plan. They had time to drum up interest across the country, and to expand their Alaskan and Canadian motives to include the entire Pacific Rim, and so to create for Seattle a "coming out party." They would open an exposition "On time in 1909" that, they schemed, would be grander than Portland, Oregon's Lewis and Clark Centennial Expo of 1905, for which there were then still

fresh impressions. The fair's chamber of boosters was content to let Portland have the Columbia River. Seattle would take the Pacific Ocean and everything it touched north and west of Astoria.

The 1893 World's Columbian Exposition in Chicago was the template for the Alaska-Yukon-Pacific Exposition, and it also influenced the 1901 Pan American Expo in Buffalo, New York; the 1904 Louisiana Purchase International Exhibit in St. Louis, Missouri; and, as noted, the Jamestown (and Norfolk), Virginia Exposition of 1907.

Following Chicago's lead, all of them emphasized the tug-of-war between the two pulls of human nature. The tug of the sublime was catered with the lavishly lit and ornamented beaux-arts classical architecture and reflecting pools. The ridiculous tilt to talking horses, thrill rides, and "human zoos" of imported aboriginals was unfurled on the Chicago fair's Midway. At the A-Y-P it found a home on the fair's brightly lighted, gaudy street of eateries and entertainments called the Pay Streak (a term used to describe the gold-bearing veins of the Klondike).

The earliest historians of the Alaska-Yukon-Pacific Exposition were vigorously nostalgic for it. Seattle's Clarence Bagley wrote in 1916, "Inspiration, courage, genius, and above all perseverance were with its leaders, and its success was remarkable, without an incident to mar the enjoyment of the casual or constant visitor." The pioneer historian must have missed the incidents of typhoid that followed a mix-up in the A-Y-P's plumbing, when the fresh and treated municipal supply was switched for raw lake water drawn to feed the landscape, not the visitors. Later historians have generally not been as kind to the tone or temper of the fair. Coll Thrush in *Crossing Over Place*, his recent book on Native Seattle history, concluded, "Like other world's fairs, the AYPE was intensely didactic, brazenly ambitious, and thoroughly racist." The Alaska-Yukon-Pacific Exposition was all of these things and more. This book reopens the gates and turns the lights back on. Welcome back to Seattle and Washington state's first world's fair.

Alaska Monument, Court of Honor, Cascade Fountain, and Geyser Basin.

BIRTH OF A FAIR

SEATTLE STRIKES IT RICH ON THE KLONDIKE GOLD RUSH OF 1897. DURING THE NEXT DECADE THE CITY BEGINS ITS TRANSFORMATION FROM BOOM TOWN TO MODERN CITY. GOVERNMENT DEALS AMBIVALENTLY WITH VICE, BUT BEGINS SPENDING ON MUCH-NEEDED INFRASTRUCTURE IMPROVEMENTS — CLEAN WATER, ELECTRICITY, BETTER TRANSIT AND STREETS. BUT HOW TO KEEP THE SETTLERS COMING AND THE MONEY ROLLING IN? AN ALASKAN VISITOR HAS AN IDEA.

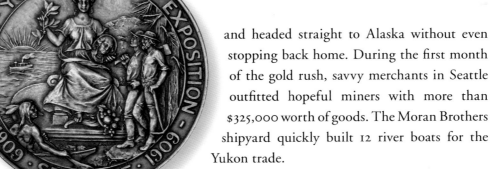

ON THE MORNING OF JULY 17, 1897, PUGET Sound residents woke to the sound of newsboys crying out the morning's headline from the *Seattle Post-Intelligencer* special edition: "Gold! Gold! Gold! Gold!" Crowds ran down to the Seattle waterfront just in time to greet the steamer *Portland*, which was carrying two tons of the precious metal mined from the banks of the Klondike River in Canada's Yukon Territory.

Within days, thousands of fortune seekers quit their jobs and scrambled to board northbound ships. William D. Wood, lawyer, land speculator, and Republican mayor of Seattle, who was attending a convention in San Francisco, telegraphed his resignation and headed straight to Alaska without even stopping back home. During the first month of the gold rush, savvy merchants in Seattle outfitted hopeful miners with more than $325,000 worth of goods. The Moran Brothers shipyard quickly built 12 river boats for the Yukon trade.

Seattle became a boom town. It was not only the "Gateway to Alaska," but also the threshold for the return trip. Lucky sourdoughs who met with success were soon trading in their gold dust and nuggets for cash and spending it throughout the city and state. By the end of the century, assayers in Seattle had exchanged more than $18 million in gold — equivalent to more than $400 million in today's inflated dollars. Much of this money was spent in Seattle and provided an enormous boost for a frontier city whose population in 1900 numbered 80,671.

ABOVE RIGHT: Alaska-Yukon-Pacific Exposition bronze medal; **LEFT:** During the Klondike gold rush, ships like the *Lucile* carried miners and their supplies from Seattle to Alaska.

OUTFITTING THE SOURDOUGHS

The monetary effects of the Klondike Gold Rush were felt in Seattle almost immediately, before most miners began traveling north. The Canadian government required every stampeder to carry a year's worth of supplies before they were allowed to cross the border from Alaska into the Yukon Territory. Since Seattle was the "Gateway to Alaska," outfitters like Schwabacher Bros. & Company and Cooper & Levy made vast fortunes long before customers tried to make theirs.

Recommended purchases included tents, ropes, axes, shovels, picks, knives, and whipsaws. Most miners bought three suits of heavy underwear, a mackinaw coat, a rubber coat, two pairs of work pants, two overalls, a dozen pairs of wool socks, six pairs of mittens, two pairs of work boots, two pairs of shoes, blankets, and mosquito netting. The bulk of weight carried was food, which generally included 400 pounds of flour, 150 pounds of bacon, 125 pounds of beans, 25 pounds of dried potatoes, 25 pounds of sugar, 15 pounds of salt, and 10 pounds of coffee.

Transporting the ton of supplies to Alaska by ship was the easy part. Getting it into Canada required Herculean effort. One person could usually carry 50 to 80 pounds at a time, which meant multiple trips over Chilkoot pass from Skagway, in Alaska, to the Yukon Territory. It was not uncommon for a single miner to walk a total 1,000 miles to carry supplies from the boat landing to his claim, about 35 miles away.

LEFT: George Carmack made the first strike in what would become the Klondike Gold Rush; TOP: Advertisement for a lecture about Alaska and the Klondike; ABOVE: Cooper & Levy at 104–106 1st Avenue S in Seattle outfitted hopeful gold miners.

ABOVE: In 1905, Seattle's Western Avenue bustled with farmers selling their produce from horse-drawn wagons. BELOW: Seattle Chamber of Commerce Executive Vice-President Ira Nadeau became A-Y-P's Director General.

MONEY TO GO AROUND

The Gold Rush erased the deprivations of the Panic of 1893, when a precipitous drop in United States gold reserves had triggered a national depression. The influx of capital led to the founding of some of Seattle's major businesses. John Nordstrom invested his golden fortune in a family shoe store (which later evolved into Nordstrom Department Store). George Bartell opened a drug store. Joshua Green, who became wealthy by transporting miners and their gear to Alaska, funneled most of his profits back into his ship-building empire.

Those who were less careful with their new-found wealth quickly discovered other ways to spend it. After Mayor Wood ran off to seek his fortune, Thomas Humes, also a Republican, was appointed to replace him in 1897. He opened the town up to saloons, casinos, and brothels, making it all the easier to separate returning miners from their gains.

The police department was soon overwhelmed. Some cops just gave in and worked in cahoots with the city's underworld, offering "protection" in exchange for cash. Illegal slot machines popped up, booze was sold to underage children, and there were even instances of men being shanghaied onto ocean-going vessels. Crime was rampant in the city's tenderloin.

But since most of the profits found their way into the wallets of Mayor Humes's backers, he won the 1900 election by a landslide. Humes promised to clean up crime, but that didn't happen.

Rapid growth put a strain on the delivery and management of essential services, so city officials invested in Seattle's infrastructure.

The Alaska Building at 2nd Avenue and Cherry Street in Seattle.

ALASKA CLUB

The Alaska Club, an organization that promoted Alaska and its resources, was formed in 1904. Housed on the 15th floor of the Alaska Building at 2nd Avenue and Cherry Street in downtown Seattle, the club offered a meeting room, a reading room, and an exhibit on Alaska in its reception area. The club also served as an information bureau, publishing *The Alaska Almanac* annually.

In 1908 the Alaska Club merged with the Arctic Club, a social organization of people from Alaska or connected with it through business. The new club, known as the Arctic Club, combined the social and business aspects of the two organizations. The Arctic Building at 3rd Avenue and Cherry Street housed their offices and gathering rooms, including the famous Dome Room. The club disbanded in 1971, most of its members having succumbed to old age, 74 years after the Gold Rush started.

The Cedar River was tapped to provide clean, plentiful water and voters approved bonds for the construction of a municipal hydroelectric dam and plant at Cedar Lake. This led to the creation of Seattle City Light, a publicly owned utility. City Engineer R. H. Thomson helped pave the way for 1907 annexations that doubled Seattle's land area by constructing major thoroughfares to outlying communities. He also set into motion an ambitious plan to grade streets and flatten hills in downtown Seattle. Rail access to the city increased thanks to the construction of the new King Street Station.

Burgeoning economic development since 1897 had been driven in large part by the Gold Rush and by Seattle's ties to Alaska and the Yukon. This got civic leaders and businessmen thinking about ways to capitalize on these links for the longer term. It was fitting that the spark they needed came from an Alaskan.

AN IDEA SNOWBALLS

Godfrey Chealander, originally from Tacoma, owned a confectionary/tobacco shop in Skagway, situated at the northern end of the Alaska panhandle, the gateway to the Klondike. In 1905, at the behest of District of Alaska Governor John Green Brady, Chealander created a display of Alaska materials for the 1905 Lewis and Clark Exposition in Portland. En route to the fair, Chealander stopped in Seattle. He was already convinced that displaying examples of Alaska's bounty had great economic merit. But he was disappointed that, having had too little time to gather materials, his display at the Lewis and Clark Exposition would not do Alaska justice. Chealander told members of Seattle's Alaska Club that Seattle might do well to host a fair highlighting Alaska — with ample time to gather examples of the region's resources.

While Chealander was busy at the Portland exposition, *The Seattle Daily Times* took up the idea of holding an Alaska fair in Seattle, printing positive editorials and trumpeting the lengthening list of prominent people who concurred. When Chealander returned from Portland, he formally presented the Executive Committee of the Alaska Club a proposal to hold an Alaska Exposition in 1907, marking the 10th anniversary of the discovery of gold in the Klondike.

In the fall of 1905, Chealander traveled through the Northwest Territories canvassing support for the idea. Yukon Territorial Governor W. W. B. McInnes proposed the inclusion of Canada's

Yukon Territory. The *Seattle Post-Intelligencer* and *The Seattle Daily Times* responded enthusiastically.

On November 10, Chealander met with the Seattle Chamber of Commerce, some of whose members also belonged to the Alaska Club. All agreed that Seattle would host a fair devoted to promoting and exploiting the resources of Alaska and the Yukon Territory from June 1, 1907, to December 1, 1907. They formed a committee charged with assessing planning needs and working out the details of incorporating an exposition company.

PICKING A DATE

The Exposition Company was formed on May 7, 1906. Fifty businessmen (and no women) composed the board of trustees. The next day the Alaska-Yukon Exposition was incorporated. The trustees elected the exposition's officers, beginning with John E. Chilberg as president. Chilberg was vice president of Seattle's Scandinavian-American Bank and president of the Alaska Club. He had engaged in mining and shipping ventures in Alaska. Other officers, all

prominent Seattle businessmen, included lawyer and former Seattle mayor Richard A. Ballinger, first vice-president; mill owner Albert S. Kerry, second vice-president; railroad agent and Seattle Chamber of Commerce officer Ira A. Nadeau, director general; engineer Charles R. Collins, treasurer; and *Seattle Daily Times* writer William M. Sheffield, secretary.

Chilberg drew from the pool of trustees, appointing men to head the following committees: executive; finance; supplies; ways and means; concessions and privileges; exhibits; transportation; rules and regulations; press and publicity; grounds and buildings; ceremonies, music, amusements and athletic sports; legislation; and mines and mining. From these committees flowed the plans that would make the exposition a reality.

TOP: A postcard featuring Chief Seattle's daughter Princess Angeline, the Pioneer Square totem pole, and other Seattle icons advertised the A-Y-P; BELOW LEFT: Visitors arriving at Seattle's waterfront in the months preceding the fair were greeted by A-Y-P staff eager to publicize the exposition; BELOW RIGHT: John Chilberg, born in Iowa and educated at Washington Territorial University, had widespread business experience in Seattle, Central America, and Alaska, and was a natural choice to head the A-Y-P.

> *"The purpose of the exposition of 1909 is the exploitation of the newly opened Northland of North America, Alaska, and Yukon, and also the two score countries bordering upon the earth's greatest ocean — the Pacific"*
>
> Frank Merrick, *Alaska-Yukon Magazine*, May 1907

But hosting the fair in 1907 proved impractical. Planning was already well underway for a Norfolk, Virginia, exposition celebrating the Jamestown settlement's tercentenary that same year. Seattle organizers realized that it would be impossible to secure federal funding for a U.S government exhibit at a second 1907 fair. Government exhibits at major expositions featured thousands of historical, political, ethnographic, and educational materials, drawing visitors and validating a fair's importance.

Opening day for the Seattle exposition was therefore shifted to June 1, 1909. This enabled fair directors to pin down the countless details necessary to pull off an exposition.

GETTING THE WORD OUT

As the Exposition Company solidified, support arose for a larger fair. On May 31, 1906, the Executive Committee announced that the fair's scope would be widened to promote countries that bordered the Pacific Ocean. As Chilberg later explained, "Because of the importance of Oriental business to Seattle, we added the name Pacific to our corporate title." A decade earlier, in August 1896, the Japanese steamship *Miiki Maru* had steamed into Elliott Bay bringing a cargo of teas, raw silk, camphor, curios, soy oil, and paper. The vessel had steamed away carrying lumber, flour, raw cotton, leather, nails, beer, wire, and tobacco. Thus began a flourishing trade between the United States and Japan, along with concurrent tensions over Hawaii, where circles of Japanese and United States expansionism intersected. Exposition officials planned

to highlight the rich resources of Hawaii (annexed by the U.S in 1898) and the Philippine Islands (under American control). They believed that if they did so, the federal government would be more likely to approve an appropriation. Securing this appropriation was crucial to the success and magnitude of the exposition. In the directors' eyes, this also made the exposition a world's fair, and thus an opportunity for many nations to celebrate (the term at the time was "exploit") their riches.

Attracting fairgoers who might move to Washington was also a goal. Portland's success in drawing Eastern visitors to the Lewis and Clark Exposition was obvious to Seattle's boosters, who planned to build A-Y-P publicity on the foundation laid by Portland, keeping the Pacific Coast in the national eye. Low railroad rates were sought to encourage Easterners to visit the fair.

Portland resident Henry E. Reed was appointed director of exploitation. Formerly secretary and director of exploitation at the 1905 Lewis and Clark Exposition in Portland, Reed did much to shape the A-Y-P Exposition planning. The divisions under him were Exploitation (which included publicity), Exhibits, Concessions, and Admissions and Works. This included soliciting participation from the U.S. government, and the governments of other nations, states, and territories.

Reed was regarded as something of an oracle. He not only had the Lewis and Clark Exposition under his belt but also had done extensive research on previous world's fairs. His first-hand knowledge of expositions gave A-Y-P planning a substantial boost.

The A-Y-P's chief of publicity, Frank L. Merrick, a reporter and son of a *Washington Post* photographer, was well versed in the fine art of fair flacking, having served as assistant to the manager of the Press Bureau at the 1904 Louisiana Purchase Exposition in St. Louis and as manager of the publicity bureau at the 1905 Lewis and Clark Exposition in Portland. Merrick poured forth articles documenting the fair's progress from the most favorable perspective. Beginning in September 1906 and extending through the opening of the exposition, Merrick edited progress reports that appeared monthly in The *Alaska-Yukon Magazine.* Merrick wrote, "The awakening of the Pacific, the transformation of the back yard of the world into the front terraces — that is what the exposition will celebrate."

Merrick churned out press releases to more than 6,500 newspapers around the world as well as to magazines and trade publications — the latter in order to attract attention from manufacturers who would, it was hoped, exhibit their goods at the A-Y-P. By May 1907, Merrick had already amassed four scrapbooks of clippings — evidence that news about the exposition was indeed spreading.

TAKING STOCK

Fair officials set a goal of selling $500,000 in shares of A-Y-P Exposition stock (shares had a par value of $10) in a single day. On October 2, 1906, Seattle not only met this goal but exceeded it, subscribing to $650,000 worth of stock in a day. This gave the city bragging rights over Portland, where a few years earlier $400,000 had been raised in 48 hours to fund the Lewis and Clark Exposition.

Many stockholders were private individuals who purchased small amounts. Businesses that hoped to profit from the fair became major stockholders. These included the railroads Northern Pacific Railway (2,500 shares) and Oregon-Washington Railroad & Navigation

ABOVE: A-Y-P Exploitation Director Henry Reed (with cane), Oregon Governor George Chamberlain (center), A-Y-P Director General Ira Nadeau (next), A-Y-P Publicity Director Frank Merrick (next), A-Y-P Director of Exhibits Henry Dosch (white beard), and A-Y-P board member Godfrey Chealander (second from right) with members of the Oregon Commission, who were responsible for the Oregon Building; **OPPOSITE PAGE:** The Pacific Northwest's natural beauty influenced the way the fair was marketed.

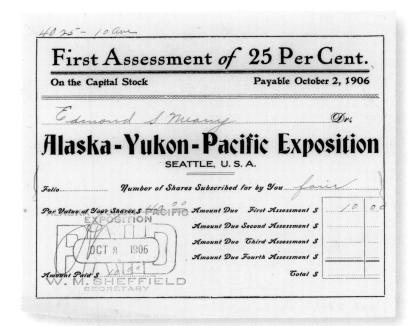

First Assessment *of* 25 Per Cent.

On the Capital Stock   Payable October 2, 1906

Edmond S Meany   Dr.

Alaska-Yukon-Pacific Exposition

SEATTLE, U.S.A.

Folio................   *Number of Shares Subscribed for by You* four

Par Value of Your Shares $................   *Amount Due   First Assessment* $ 10 00

                          Amount Due   Second Assessment $

                          Amount Due   Third Assessment $

                          Amount Due   Fourth Assessment $

Amount Paid $................   *Total* $

W. M. SHEFFIELD
SECRETARY

TOP: Edmond Meany's first assessment for A-Y-P stock;
BOTTOM: Beloved University of Washington history professor
Edmond Meany played a crucial role in planning and guiding
the A-Y-P.

Company (2,500 shares); newspapers *Seattle Post-Intelligencer* (2,000 shares), *The Seattle Times* (2,000 shares), and Star Publishing, owner of the *Seattle Star* (1,000 shares); Seattle Brewing and Malting (999 shares); the electric and transportation utility Stone & Webster (1,500 shares); a coal mining enterprise that also manufactured cement and owned an island in Alaska for quarrying lime, the Pacific Coast Company (1,000 shares); and building contractors Strehlow, Freese & Peterson (777 1/2 shares).

FAIR SITES

The University of Washington grounds were chosen for the exposition over Magnolia Bluff, Mount Baker Park, Bailey Peninsula (now Seward Park), Woodland Park, and Washington Park (now the Washington Park Arboretum). Col. Alden J. Blethen, influential publisher of *The Seattle Daily Times* and a former University of Washington regent, pushed for the university site, as did the state senator from Walla Walla, W. J. Pauly.

Many preferred the university site for its beauty, sanitary conditions, size, and transportation that would be adequate after improvements. Site selection committee member Edmond Meany — a leading University of Washington professor who always had the school's best interest in mind — also seized upon the possibility that, unlike other expositions where buildings were constructed to last through the fair and no more, at least some buildings created for the A-Y-P Exposition could be permanent additions to the campus and thus relieve crowded conditions that the state Legislature had been unwilling to remedy.

One potential financial issue with the selected site was that the sale of liquor, a big money-maker at other exhibitions, was forbidden by law within two miles of the University of Washington campus. Thus, the A-Y-P Exposition would become the only dry world's fair in history.

PROPERTY MANAGEMENT

The lease between the University of Washington Board of Regents and the Alaska-Yukon-Pacific Exposition Company extended from October 2, 1906, to January 1, 1910. Existing buildings in use by the university were exempted from the lease. The Exposition Company was not charged for use of the property, and in turn it did not charge a site fee to the counties, states, and countries wishing to erect buildings for the fair. Neither did it charge a fee for mounting exhibits in other buildings.

The Washington Legislature appropriated $1 million to sponsor the exposition, $600,000 of which was designated to erect four permanent buildings to be used by the university after the fair. University President Thomas Kane and the Board of Regents decided that these buildings would house chemistry, engineering, an auditorium, and a power plant. During the fair the future Chemistry Building was used as the Fine Arts Building and the future Engineering Building was used as the Machinery Building.

Although other exposition buildings survived and were utilized by the university for varying periods, these four were specifically funded, designed, and constructed to be permanent. The remaining $400,000 would fund construction of the Washington State Building and its exhibits, including the expense of collecting and maintaining the exhibits.

RAISING CAPITAL

Director of Exploitation Henry Reed sent A-Y-P Special Commissioner Major T. S. Clark on a long and arduous trip to present the exposition officially to the governors of every state. A dozen special commissioners were also in the field working hard to

The official Alaska-Yukon-Pacific Exposition flag.

secure the support of the states. A-Y-P Director General Ira Nadeau, meanwhile, traveled to Canada to officially invite the Dominion Government's participation. Canadian officials delayed making this commitment until the U.S. government's participation had been decided — which, as it turned out, took quite some time.

The push for federal government participation began in late 1906 when the fair corporation asked Washington's senatorial delegation to work for a $1 million appropriation for buildings and exhibits. President Theodore Roosevelt backed federal participation in his annual address to Congress. The Senate passed a bill during the 1907 session authorizing $700,000, but the House failed to act.

During the next congressional session, anxious fair officials traveled to Washington, D.C., to assist Washington senators Samuel Piles and Levi Ankeny, both Republicans, in lobbying legislators. The Jamestown Exposition had done so poorly that its officials had defaulted on $860,000 of the $1 million they borrowed from the federal government. Fooled once, Congress was twice shy.

Influential Seattleites called in favors. Edmond Meany worked steadily behind the scenes to secure the federal government appropriation that would fund the government buildings and the hundreds of educational exhibits they would house. He wrote letters beseeching friends, who

THE UNIVERSITY OF WASHINGTON AND THE UNIVERSITY DISTRICT

BEFORE THE A-Y-P

On November 4, 1861, the Territorial University opened in downtown Seattle on a four-block area of land donated by Arthur Denny. The university was located on what is now the site of the Olympic Hotel with 30 students and one teacher. Hopes were high but funding was a problem from the very start. The university closed briefly in 1866 for lack of money, and the first collegiate degree wasn't awarded until 1876, when Clara McCarty accepted her Bachelor of Science diploma.

After Washington achieved statehood in 1889, the Legislature decided that a new campus was needed away from downtown where the university could grow accordingly. In 1895, the University of Washington opened at its present site along Lake Washington. Denny Hall and the observatory were some of the first buildings to open and both still stand today, as does Parrington Hall, built in 1902.

When the A-Y-P opened, other buildings on the campus north of the fairgrounds included the chimes tower, a men's dormitory, a women's dormitory, and a gymnasium.

The Territorial University as it looked twenty years after its building in 1861.

DEVELOPMENT IN THE DISTRICT

As grounds were groomed and buildings rose on the exposition site, family houses sprouted like dandelions on recently platted lots in the fledgling neighborhoods surrounding the university. The *Seattle Post-Intelligencer* ran a full page of classified advertisements for university-area lots and houses under the heading "University District, Where Investors Are Busy." The paper stated, "The great amount of building in the University district is due undoubtedly to the A-Y-P. It has drawn thousands of people out there on sightseeing trips. Many of these had just arrived in the city and were seeking for property on which to build homes. The great natural advantages of the district appealed to many, and they are starting homes."

Ravenna Park Heights, Exposition Heights, University Park Addition, University Scenic Addition, A. B. Graham's University Addition, and many other larger parcels that make up parts of the University District, Ravenna, and Laurelhurst neighborhoods, were subdivided into individual lots. These properties were adorned with cottages, four-squares, bungalows, stores, hotels, and apartment buildings as the A-Y-P Exposition and its concurrent improvements to roads, public transportation, and infrastructure stimulated community expansion.

THE CAMPUS

The lay of the land on the University of Washington campus in 1908–1909 varied substantially from the modern campus. Padelford Hall and the attached parking structure sit in the Natural Amphitheatre that the exposition used for speeches and musical performances. Lake Washington reached all the way to just below the amphitheater, about where Montlake Boulevard runs today. On the south end of campus, no ship canal bisected the portage between Capitol Hill and the lower campus. Instead, the University Extension, a broad boulevard, crossed the portage through the forest between the lakes to connect with Lake Washington Boulevard.

IMPROVEMENTS

Before the University of Washington grounds were chosen as the A-Y-P site, the Brooklyn neighborhood, now known as the University District, had few city services. Just one streetcar line served the neighborhood, and dirt roads, muddy in the winter and dusty in the summer,

prevailed. In the year leading up to the exposition, the area gained three streetcar lines, one that ran from downtown to the exposition, following 23rd Avenue, and another that crossed the newly widened Latona Bridge, where the Interstate 5 Ship Canal Bridge is today, and followed 40th Street across to 14th Avenue, which is now University Way. The third ran from Ballard over to Fremont, then joined the Wallingford line to the university.

A new road, the University Extension, connected the campus with Lake Washington

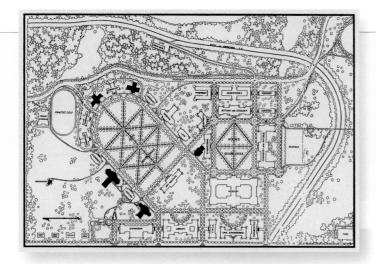

Boulevard over the portage that still separated Lakes Washington and Union, providing a scenic route for automobile traffic to the exposition. The area also gained a new sewer line, sidewalks, and street paving. Although welcome, these improvements also caused hardship for neighborhood residents. Any street improvement costs had to be paid by the adjacent property owners, up to a certain limit, so they each received a bill for their portion of the costs. The Seattle Electric Company, which ran the streetcar lines, paid for the lines they added, including the passenger sheds built at 40th Street and 14th Avenue.

ABOVE CENTER: **Brooklyn neighborhood (later University District), ca. 1906.**

CLOCKWISE FROM FAR LEFT: **Territorial University, Seattle, ca. 1881; Denny Hall, University of Washington, n.d.; The Olmsted Brothers' 1904 University of Washington campus plan was not adopted; A-Y-P grounds prior to construction; Observatory, University of Washington, 1896; Chimes Tower, University of Washington, n.d.**

"A great exposition is a great national educator. The thousands and tens of thousands of people who are able to take a holiday and to visit an exposition, view with admiration and pride the handwork of their fellowmen, the geniousness of their conception in art, industry, science and education. They view the splendid exhibits, the stately and magnificent exposition palaces, surpassing in beauty of architecture even King Solomon's temple itself — in short, they view the mammoth work of man in every line of endeavor, and in a few days time they have seen more, and learned more and received greater education, and a more practical knowledge of the country's and the world's progress and development, than would have been possible from a lifetime study of books. They go back home contented and satisfied. In their hearts has been instilled a desire to become better men, better women and better children, intent upon striving for something higher than their former usual wont — to try to achieve and to emulate the examples of others for that which is good and ennobling; and the nation profits for this education, for a better standard for citizenship has been molded."

Godfrey Chealander, *Alaska-Yukon Magazine,* August 1907

ABOVE: A-Y-P boosters purchased formal invitations to send to friends;
OPPOSITE PAGE: Jamestown Exposition logo.

in turn lobbied the legislators. Federal money was also required to underwrite buildings and ex-hibits for Alaska, Hawaii, and the Philippines. Henry Reed and former Washington Governor John H. McGraw were in Washington, D.C., lob-bying Congress for a $700,000 appropriation. Once Exposition President Chilberg had secured Washington state funds, he joined them in this effort.

Both as a point of pride and as a marketing tool, A-Y-P Exposition officials made much of the fact that their petition to Congress was for an appropriation to fund the federal government's own exhibits, not a general grant or a loan. Both the Jamestown Exposition and the Louisiana Purchase Exposition used congressional gifts and loans over and above the government's own build-ings and exhibits, a practice that opened these expositions to public criticism.

Over and over again A-Y-P Exposition officials stressed that any federal funding would be spent by government-appointed committees to build facili-ties and gather items for dis-play, and that the Washington state appropriation was being disbursed by a committee appointed by Governor Albert E. Mead, not by exposition officials. The only funds controlled by the A-Y-P Exposition were the funds subscribed to by Seattle citizens, gate receipts, and concession profits.

FROM THE GROUND UP

The Olmsted Brothers landscape architecture firm of Brookline, Massachusetts, was selected to plan the fairgrounds. John C. Olmsted had laid out the grounds of the World's Columbian Exposition in Chicago and the Lewis and Clark Exposition in Portland, as well as the 1903 master plan for Seattle's 20-mile greensward of parks. In 1904 his firm had prepared a plan for the university's future expansion, but the Legislature had decreed it too costly and funded no construction at that time.

Olmsted's preliminary plan for the A-Y-P grounds included extensive use of the land all the way to the Lake Washington waterfront, but this was deemed too expensive. His next version reduced space between buildings, and placed the majority of the grounds inside the ring created by railroad tracks that circled the lower part of the campus. This meant less grading work, shorter roads, and fewer sidewalks, which helped keep the plan within the $380,000 budget. Olmsted spent six months delineating all exposition features. The plan was executed under the oversight of John Olmsted's collaborator James Frederick Dawson.

The A-Y-P grounds were situated between Lake Union and Lake Washington, and planned for both were canoe races, motor boat races, and swimming and diving championships. (The Lake Washington Ship Canal joining the two lakes had yet to be dug). The Olmsted grounds plan included a large athletic field with grandstands and bleachers to seat thousands. Dreaming big, exposition officials envisioned world championships in polo, lacrosse, baseball, Rugby, football, and basketball.

The A-Y-P also envisioned hosting what Frank Merrick termed the "primordial sports of the Alaskan and Yukon natives," the first exposition to showcase these activities. Plans included foot races, archery, walrus-spearing, bidarka (Aleut canoe) racing, and many other forms of "primitive competition."

As grounds plans were solidified, UW President Thomas Kane urged planners to remember that the building arrangements must suit the university after the fair as well as benefit the A-Y-P. Kane pushed for the permanent buildings to be located on the northern part of campus nearer to existing buildings. The southern campus, closer to Lake Union's odors and soggy wetlands, was less desirable.

PROMOTING A-Y-P AT THE JAMESTOWN EXPOSITION

Lloyd W. McDowell, secretary of the Alaska-Yukon-Pacific Exposition Commission at Jamestown, promoted the A-Y-P to Jamestown, Virginia, fairgoers. Many, he discovered, were of modest means but planned ahead for summer travel. Unsure exactly where in the wild, wild West Seattle figured, fairgoers queried McDowell about how close Seattle was to the Mexican border, whether it was situated across the bay from San Francisco, and which train routes to take to see Yellowstone National Park en route. This last was completely possible, and rail lines and steam ship companies lost no time in adding A-Y-P promotions to their advertisements.

McDowell's one-on-one promotional efforts and free literature were supplemented by the ballyhoo at The Klondike placer goldmine, a popular attraction on the Warpath, the Jamestown Exposition's midway area. Klondike operator P. R. Ritchie, dressed as an Alaskan miner, regaled crowds with stories of Seattle and the upcoming A-Y-P before leading them into the replica placer mine where he simulated gold mining. The Department of Agriculture Building and Army and Navy Building also featured educational exhibits about Alaska, and these whetted the Jamestown fairgoers' appetites for the A-Y-P.

John Galen Howard of the San Francisco architecture firm Howard & Galloway was given charge of building design. The Olmsted firm had envisioned fair buildings modeled after traditional Russian architecture, a nod to Alaska's settlement by Russians. Howard & Galloway favored a less exotic neoclassical approach. Four Seattle architecture firms, Bebb & Mendel, Saunders & Lawton, Graham & Meyers, and Schack & Huntington, were retained as advisors.

Architect and engineer Frank P. Allen Jr. was appointed the A-Y-P's director of works. Allen immediately began planning the massive work of clearing forest, grading, and filling specified in John C. Olmsted's design. Olmsted urged Allen to spare medium-sized Douglas fir trees and their

undergrowth where possible, although this increased expense. Some of the trees preserved were as tall as 250 feet.

CITY CHANGES

Seattle, meanwhile, was undergoing a transformation of its own — from a Wild West town into a modern metropolis. In 1907, Mayor William Hickman Moore, a Democrat, oversaw the annexation of six communities that expanded city boundaries in all directions. Beginning on January 7, the city annexed Southeast Seattle, which included the neighborhoods of Seward Park, Mt. Baker, Beacon Hill, and a portion of Rainier Valley. Eight days later, Ravenna was annexed to the north. Columbia City, South Park, and Ballard joined in May, and West Seattle followed in July.

The city expanded upward as well as outward. The year 1907 welcomed the opening of the new Pike Place Market, new schools, new houses of worship, a new theater, a new amusement park,

TOP: Architectural rendering of the Fine Arts Building; BOTTOM: As A-Y-P Director of Works, architect and engineer Frank Allen Jr. managed all work done on the grounds before and during the exposition; OPPOSITE PAGE: Montlake ditch from Lake Washington to Portage Bay, February 22, 1902.

a children's hospital, and a new-fangled shop called a "gas station" — one of the first in the world.

Attempts were made to curb some of the vice that resulted from the open-town policies of previous administrations. Mayor Moore saw to it that saloons were closed on Sundays, but he dragged his feet when it came to shutting down gambling houses.

Exploitation Director Henry Reed advised exposition trustees that Seattle should begin preparing itself to be "the hostess of the world in 1909" — beautifying streets and creating new ones, clearing alleys of rubbish, and building infrastructure to support hundreds of thousands of fair visitors. The Board of Park Commissioners made a special effort to have the chain of landscaped boulevards along or overlooking Lake Washington open for traffic. The views, they predicted, would stun Eastern visitors.

The state provided funding by deciding to sell some state-owned shore lands on both Lake Washington and Lake Union.

BREAKING BREAD, BREAKING GROUND

People perusing the *Seattle Post-Intelligencer* on April 1, 1907, may have spluttered their coffee at the headline "Mr. Nadeau Eats Rats For Supper." The story was no April Fool's joke. Proving beyond any doubt his determination to promote A-Y-P, Director General Ira Nadeau, who was traveling the country telling civic organizations about the fair, broke bread — and muskrat — with yacht club members in his hometown of Monroe, Michigan, then gave a speech about the A-Y-P. This muskrat feast was (and remains) an annual event.

May 8, 1907, marked the first anniversary of the fair's incorporation, and on June 1, 1907, ground was broken, signaling the beginning of the two-year push to make the exposition's advertising tag line — "The World's Most Beautiful Exposition. The World's Fair That Will Be Ready" — a reality. Being Ready would establish credibility — and would distinguish the A-Y-P from many other expositions that were only partially completed when they opened their gates.

The festivities started at noon with a military parade through downtown Seattle to Union Station, where a special train waited to carry dignitaries and the crowd to the exposition grounds. Once at the fairgrounds, the crowd, fair publicist Frank Merrick wrote,

ADELAIDE HANSCOM'S A-Y-P LOGO

Adelaide Hanscom, born in Empire City (now Coos Bay), Oregon, in 1875, and reared primarily in Berkeley, California, worked as a painter, illustrator, and later photographer from the time she was in her late teens. Her photography studio on Market Street in San Francisco was destroyed during the San Francisco earthquake and fire of April 18, 1906, and Hanscom moved to Seattle in September 1906. For the next year she worked primarily as a photographer of Seattle's high society, and her photographic portraits of women and children were featured in local newspapers.

In July 1907 the A-Y-P publicity committee unanimously selected Hanscom's graceful circular design as the official A-Y-P logo over several hundred other entries. Although her photographic work had been awarded medals in exhibitions and her illustrations for *The Rubaiyat of Omar Khayyam* were well known, the A-Y-P competition was the first such contest Hanscom had ever entered. She received $500 in prize money.

Hanscom described the significance of the emblem's three female figures: "The figure to the right typifies the Pacific slope with right hand extended in welcome and the left holding a train of cars representing commerce by land. The figure to the left represents the Orient, and the ship in her hand represents commerce by sea. The central figure in white is that of Alaska, the white representing the North and the nuggets in her hand representing her vast mineral resources."

Unlike the emblems of other expositions, the A-Y-P logo was purposely not copyrighted, enabling its free use by anyone wishing to promote or profit from the exposition.

Adelaide Hanscom's logo appeared in paint (top), print (detail, left), cloisonné (center), and plaster (right).

"stood, sat, or reclined on [the Natural Amphitheatre's] grassy slopes during the three hours of speech-making … . Mingling with the brightness of the women's summer gowns and the men's dull attire was the dash of color of the soldiers. On the outer edge of the amphitheatre were automobiles and carriages filled with smart-dressed women and well-groomed men."

Here and there large banners bearing the names of states proclaimed that state societies were in attendance. State societies were composed of individuals who had moved to the Pacific Northwest but still liked to affiliate with others from their home states. They lobbied their home state legislatures to secure appropriations and to plan their state's A-Y-P participation. Counties, states, and foreign countries that did not erect their own buildings could have their displays in other exhibit buildings.

More than 15,000 people gathered to watch President Chilberg turn the first shovel of earth. President Theodore Roosevelt sent John Barrett, director of the International Bureau of American Republics and a former West Coast newspaperman, to represent him at the ceremonies. Press accounts of the event make it clear that VIPs from throughout the Pacific Northwest were present, along with a stage packed with exposition directors and University of Washington regents, most sporting fedoras and even top hats. Frank Merrick summed up the symbolism: "Typical of the riches of the countries the exposition will be held to exploit, a golden shovel and pick were used to break the ground."

The crowd listened to the speeches and then, excited to the point of frenzy, surged forward to grab clumps of earth, filling purses and pockets with the now-historic soil. They ripped from their moorings bunting, ribbons, and small flags decorating the grandstand. These instant mementos disappeared into the crowd,

presumably to be treasured in shacks, bungalows, and mansions across Seattle. Some fair enthusiasts even attempted to purloin the golden pick and shovel.

That same day Washington Governor Albert Mead convened the first meeting of the Washington State Alaska-Yukon-Pacific Exposition Commission. This commission was charged with overseeing the state's participation in the A-Y-P. Members included Judge M. M. Goodman of Dayton; H. A. McLean, a lawyer from Mount Vernon; E. G. Dickson of Ellensburg, who had served in the state Legislature; Louis P. Hornberger, of Spokane, also a former member of the state Legislature; Senator R. W. Condon of Port Gamble, director of the Puget Mill Company; Lewis H. Burnett of Grays Harbor, founder of a jewelry enterprise with several branches; and J. W. Slayden of Tacoma, also a former legislator.

TRANSFORMING THE LANDSCAPE

Workers with horse-drawn wagons began swarming over the wooded campus, felling trees, clearing stumps, and leveling ground. University students and professors attempted to ignore the dynamite

A-Y-P president John Chilberg breaks ground for the exposition, June 1, 1907.

LABOR RELATIONS

Labor unions threatened to boycott the exposition in retaliation for the hiring of non-union labor. When the city hired a firm to build a welcome arch on 2nd Avenue, unions filed for injunctions because of non-union labor that the contractor sought to hire. The injunctions only succeeded in delaying the project. In reality, a large number of union workers helped construct the fair's structures despite the open-shop practices.

Labor Day 1909 gave the unions an opportunity to express their opposition to the exposition's labor policies by not attending Seattle Day at the fair. Instead, labor leaders planned a large parade in downtown Seattle, followed by a picnic in Woodland Park. So many union members joined the parade that it took an hour to pass. When the Plasterers, Painters and Carpenters reached the Welcome Arch they fell out of line, bypassed the arch, then retook their place on the other side. Tens of thousands of union members and their families enjoyed the rest of the day at Woodland Park, picnicking, listening to bands, and playing in athletic competitions.

Construction workers and plasterers put the finishing touches on giant planter urns that would be placed throughout the fairgrounds.

blasts that rattled windows and shuddered classroom walls. The buildings planned as permanent were the first to be erected while the avenues, circles, plazas, and courts were all under construction. By November, the Administration Building was finished and occupied by the exposition staff. The massive job of clearing brush and stumps continued. The *Alaska-Yukon Magazine* stated, "At present great fires are burning on all portions of the ground, consuming the wood cut down to make room for the many buildings in the course of construction, but when these have cleared away the rubbish on the grounds the beauty of the view can be plainly seen."

Fair contractors were not required to hire union labor, and in January 1908 the Washington Federation of Labor passed a resolution calling for a boycott. It was more formality than reality — most of the men who worked on the grounds during the build-up to the fair were union members, and many ignored the boycott and later enjoyed the fair with their families.

A workforce of more than 500 was busily building both permanent and temporary structures all across the A-Y-P grounds. By spring 1908, the basin for the Arctic Circle geyser fountain (located at today's Drumheller Fountain) was completed and the Cascade Court, through which impressive artificial rapids would course, was nearly finished. The massive Manufactures Building and Agriculture Building, each of which would feature about 100,000 square feet of floor space, were still under construction. In the southeast portion of the fairgrounds, two spur tracks with minor branches were laid from the Northern Pacific Railway line onto A-Y-P grounds so that construction materials could be delivered directly.

With so many construction workers swarming the exposition grounds, the potential for accident, illness, or injury was heightened. Exposition officials made the early construction of the Hospital Building a priority. Staffed from the time it was completed in March 1908, the hospital handled emergencies during most of the building period and throughout the A-Y-P Exposition.

More than 200 men under the direction of contractor William Doyle labored to build the sewer system, planned to serve the exposition and then the University of Washington and the surrounding neighborhood. The excavations for the sewer system ranged from 5 to 30 feet underground.

In the 100-foot-long greenhouse, 15 gardeners labored over a half-million shrubs that would grace the landscaped grounds. Many were propagated from cuttings on site. The 20 acres that surrounded the greenhouse were set aside to produce annuals, grasses, and perennials that would be transplanted throughout the fair, providing swaths of color. Scarlet geraniums alone numbered some 50,000.

EXHIBITS AND AMUSEMENTS

Exposition officials primarily wanted exhibits that demonstrated how an article was made from start to finish. By March 1908 they had secured agricultural machinery, demonstrations of refrigerator, locomotive, and stationery manufacture, and a large iron foundry that would create novelty items in full public view. Demonstrations of butter and cream manufacture, machine-woven lace, commercial wool spinning and weaving, and fish-curing and packaging — including a recently invented mechanized fish-cleaning process — had already been secured more than a year before opening day. All of these exhibits would be staffed by demonstrator/educators who were prepared to explain and answer questions.

Director of Exhibits Henry Dosch was an experienced exposition commissioner from Oregon. Dosch received enquiries from many leading American manufacturers, allowing him to be selective

BELOW TOP: Seattle Engineering Company workers raise the flagpole on Dome Circle; **BELOW BOTTOM:** Exposition grounds were cleared of stumps and leveled before building construction could begin; **BELOW RIGHT:** Manufactures Building nearing completion.

PLANTINGS

John C. Olmsted, who created the landscape plan for the exposition grounds, sought to add to the natural beauty of the campus and its surroundings rather than making the plantings the focal point. The landscaping on the 250 acres varied from tidied-up forest with five miles of trails to formal gardens, with extensive informal plantings around buildings.

The work started with 20 acres of nursery grounds on the southern end of the campus. In October 1907, with 10 acres of sod seeded and a 30 by 100 foot greenhouse built, the gardeners began by gathering 194,000 plants. Propagation yielded hundreds of thousands of starts from these original plants. Additionally, several plant companies lent many thousands of plants and bulbs to the fair and a large number of plants and trees from the campus forest were saved and transplanted after the graders finished sculpting the grounds. In all, the landscaping crews planted about two million annuals, perennials, hedges, shrubs, and trees.

in assigning firms prominent spots in the Manufactures Building. He also prepared a pamphlet detailing the rules and regulations for demonstrations and displays at the A-Y-P Exposition and distributed it to interested firms.

Educational exhibits were well-meaning, but the midway — packed with rides, vaudeville acts, geegaws, and flim-flam — was expected to draw fairgoers like a magnet. Chicago had the Midway Plaisance, Saint Louis had the Pike, Portland had the Trail, and for the A-Y-P Exposition, Seattle planned the Pay Streak — named for the mining term describing the location of the richest ore.

Finding suitable concessions for the Pay Streak was a formidable task. The stated aim of educating the public and providing trustworthy exhibits meant "no fakirs, no grafters, and all shows clean." As at other major expositions, the subjective question of what constituted legitimate display of human beings, not to mention clean entertainment, was ripe for public scrutiny.

Mindful that a fair called Alaska-Yukon-Pacific had an obvious mandate to demonstrate life in Alaska, the Pay Streak would feature an exhibit of "three kinds of Eskimo, those that have not been touched by white civilization, those who only recently came into association with modern civilization, and the common or garden variety, the natives who were long ago brought into contact with white men."

At President Kane's request, the University Board of Regents added an ethnology class tailored to take advantage of the fair, bringing Dr. A. C. Haddon of Cambridge, England, to campus to teach "Stages of Cultural Evolution Around the Pacific" during the 1909 summer school session.

The Executive Committee decided to hold a livestock show during the latter part of the exposition, budgeting $100,000 for expenses and prizes. The goals were to attract the attention of breeders from around the world and to showcase the products of Northwest breeders, with special emphasis on the federal government's livestock breeding experiments underway in Alaska. Real-estate developer

LEFT: Formal gardens showcased thousands of plants and eye-popping electric-light fixtures; Featured in portraits are John Olmsted (top) and James Frederick Dawson; **OPPOSITE PAGE:** Most A-Y-P buildings took two or three months to design and four or five months to build. Agriculture Building under construction, March 19, 1908.

ABOVE LEFT: Spokane County marked its building site with an enormous billboard; **ABOVE RIGHT**: Groundbreaking ceremonies for the Swedish Building, February 29, 1909; **OPPOSITE PAGE**: Several groups of young women posed in living tableaux of the A-Y-P logo before and during the exposition. Left to right: Leah Miller, Grace Geary, Nova Taylor.

(and later founder of a model dairy farm), James W. Clise was put in charge of the A-Y-P livestock committee. Serving under him were Charles D. Stimson, D. Edward Frederick, and Theodore N. Haller of Seattle and William H. Paulhamus of Puyallup. The Executive Committee hoped that, given the two-year lead, exhibitors would breed stock especially for display at the A-Y-P.

By April 1908, Director of Exhibits Dosch reported that 50 percent of the entire exhibit space was allocated and he expected to allocate the rest within 90 days. Director of Concessions A. W. Lewis told *Alaska-Yukon Magazine* that 10 of the 30 large concessions had been let, along with hundreds of smaller concessions. These included the Eskimo Village, which would cover more than an acre of ground, the Baby Incubator exhibit, the Oriental concession, "The Creation," "Fighting the Flames" (put on by the Seattle Fire Show Company), the Bohemia Restaurant, the photographic concession to Nome-based photographer Frank H. Nowell, and a contract with Joseph Meyer & Brothers of Seattle to manufacture souvenir spoons and with Burnett Brothers of Seattle to sell them.

DOING THEIR PART

The A-Y-P Exposition Executive Committee and Board of Trustees oversaw committees that planned and facilitated every aspect of the fair. Although there were no women among these august boosters, the *Alaska-Yukon-Pacific Exposition Directory*, published in 1909, included the married men's wives and occasionally their sisters and daughters. This may have been because the directory functioned as a Social Blue Book of the fair and was used when creating guest lists for the many dinners, parties, and ceremonies that went along with hosting the exposition. It also seems to indicate that, like so many endeavors in which men manned the masthead on official stationery and stood shoulder to shoulder for official photographs, successfully conjuring the A-Y-P Exposition was a family affair.

As buildings rose, the work of committees whose job it was to fill them with exhibits intensified. These committees planned each feature of their various exhibits, and how to get specimens to the fair and keep them attractive for more than four months. For agricultural exhibits, this meant planning how and when to replenish heaps of fruit and how to keep vermin at bay. For machinery exhibits, most of which were operational demonstrations and many of which had to be shipped to Seattle from across the country, the means of power had to be available: electric, steam, water, hydraulic, or compressed air. For craft demonstrations such as hand embroidery or weaving, the silks, looms, wools, and the demonstrators themselves had to be transported from their native lands. For stock exhibits, working with top Western breeders, transporting the animals — from chickens and geese to massive steers — and housing them safely required prodigious planning. Preparations were steady but the process must have seemed endless.

On May 27, 1908, the federal government at long last appropriated $600,000 for participation in the A-Y-P Exposition. Of that, $250,000 went toward the large Government Building — designed by federal architects under the supervising architect of the Treasury — a Life Saving Station exhibit, and smaller buildings for Alaska, Hawaii, and the Philippines. The remaining $350,000

was allocated for exhibits to fill those buildings: $200,000 for the Government Building, $100,000 for Alaska, $25,000 for Hawaii, and $25,000 for the Philippines. The exhibits included facsimiles of historic documents, congressional peace medals, a model irrigated farm, giant models of crop-destroying insects, among many other items, displays, and demonstrations, most of them drawn from the collections of the Smithsonian Institution and National Museum. Assistant Secretary of the Interior Jesse E. Wilson chaired the three-person Federal Government Board of Managers. The other members were William E. Geddes of the Treasury Department and W. de C. Ravenel, administrative assistant at the National Museum.

It is impossible to overstate the degree of relief A-Y-P Exposition planners must have felt when federal funds were secured. The Olmsted plan had reserved the choicest spot for a massive Government Building, and without the federal government's participation the fair would have amounted to little more than regional boosterism.

THE ROSE CARNIVAL PARADE

On June 2, 1908, a floral parade float promoting the A-Y-P Exposition represented Seattle in the Portland, Oregon, Rose Carnival Parade. The parade's theme was Spirit of the Golden West, and the A-Y-P Exposition float was its highlight. A-Y-P Exposition managers, members of the Seattle City Council, and a crowd of 90,000 watched from the sidelines as the horse-drawn floral tribute rolled past. Three young women from Seattle topped the float, forming a living tableau of Adelaide Hanscom's logo for the fair. The float also featured a model of an exposition palace, an operational water wheel, and miniature representations of various industries. The A-Y-P sent another living logo float to the 1909 Portland Rose Festival Parade.

Portland held its first rose show in 1889 and its first floral parade on June 10, 1904. In 1907 the Portland Rose Festival was initiated using stock dividends from the Portland's 1905 Lewis and Clark Exposition. Portland became known as the City of Roses, and the Portland Rose Festival celebrated its centennial in June 2008.

FIRST LOOKS

Visiting the exposition grounds to check on progress became a major pastime for Seattle residents. Crowds took advantage of increased service on streetcar lines to attend such events as a band concert held during May 1908 Fleet Week in the Natural Amphitheatre. In July the *Alaska-Yukon Magazine* reported that more than 7,500 people visited the exposition grounds on Sundays if the weather was nice. Initially this fun was free, but beginning September 20, a 10-cent fee was charged to enter the grounds. By the time the fair opened, the dimes collected amounted to $30,212.

By the end of the summer, some of the country's leading showmen had secured concessions on the Pay Streak, which was now planned to stretch for more than a half-mile to accommodate attractions as large as the re-enacted Battle of Gettysburg and as small as the many tiny souvenir stands that would offer fairgoers ample ways to part with their pennies. The large twin Manufactures and Agriculture buildings were complete, and the geyser fountain was nearly so — its water supply had already been turned on.

The Machinery Building, one of three brick buildings planned to be permanent after the fair, was finished and the other two, the Fine Arts and Auditorium buildings, were rising steadily. The Mines Building was hiring staff, the Oregon Building was nearly complete, and ground had been broken for the California Building. Work on the Washington, New York, and Utah buildings would soon begin. So many exhibit applications had been received that two additional buildings were added to the plan: one for transportation and one for foreign exhibits. The Machinery Building gained an annex.

BELOW: On March 27, 1909, Seattle schoolchildren were invited to tour the grounds of the almost-ready exposition; **OPPOSITE PAGE:** The Oriental Building (left), Manufactures Building (right), and Cascade Fountain (foreground) during construction, October 1908.

Finally, in August 1908, Sydney Fischer, minister of agriculture at Ottawa, Canada, accepted the invitation to participate in the A-Y-P Exposition. Fischer noted that Canada would erect a building in which each province, especially the Yukon, British Columbia, Alberta, and Saskatchewan, would be represented. Coming so late in the planning period, Canada's sign-on was also an immense relief to exposition officials.

The U.S. Department of State forwarded the A-Y-P Exposition managers' invitation for participation to all diplomatic officers of the United States. A cover letter instructed them to extend this invitation to the government and people of their countries of residence. It clarified that the exposition was not under the auspices or control of the federal government, but that the government was participating. It seems likely that if the federal appropriation had been secured in 1907 as originally hoped, this sanctioned invitation to other countries would have gone out much earlier and perhaps many more countries would have erected buildings.

On September 16, 1908, members of the American Association of Traveling Passenger Agents spent the day cruising Puget Sound. Entertained on the fairgrounds and thoroughly briefed about the upcoming fair during their convention, these railroad agents — who were well versed in previous expositions — departed Seattle ready to market the A-Y-P Exposition to their numerous clients.

Three days later, A-Y-P Exposition stockholders met on the fairgrounds for a progress report. They toured the grounds, noting the many buildings that were already complete. Officials stressed that work on the A-Y-P Exposition was — for

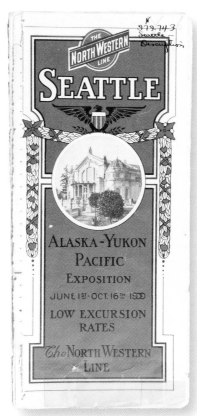
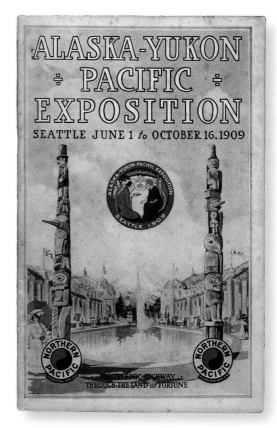

Promotional postcards and pamphlets, some distributed by railroad companies whose lines served Seattle, spread the word about the exposition.

corresponding dates — six months ahead of the progress made during construction of the Lewis and Clark Exposition and a full year ahead of the Jamestown Exposition.

By September 1908 many Pay Streak concessions managers were overseeing construction of the buildings that would house their attractions. Only the larger Pay Streak attractions were listed on the official ground plan, but contemporary photographs make it clear that smaller attractions were sited between the larger ones. Some of these smaller concessions came and went over the course of the fair, depending on their success and in order to draw repeat visitors seeking fresh thrills.

FINE TUNING

In October 1908, the Exposition Company asked the public to subscribe to $350,000 worth of bonds, to be secured by a mortgage on fair admission receipts. That year a national financial panic had hit, and raising this money proved difficult. Only a public announcement that the fair might have to be scrapped rallied the funding. Private investors put up $182,000 and banks put up the rest.

Despite his important role shaping exposition planning, Exploitation Director Henry Reed found himself squabbling more and more with the Executive Committee over his methods and salary. He tendered his resignation, and was replaced by James A. Wood, city editor at *The Seattle Daily Times* and a key early booster of the exposition.

By fall, the sewers, water mains, and electrical conduits were in place. These would be permanent and benefit the university after the fair. Gas lines were being installed, after which asphalt would be laid down over the 11 miles of streets and walkways that crisscrossed the grounds. Several miles of meandering cinder paths had been created through stands of virgin trees that the Olmsted plan had retained on the eastern periphery of the grounds.

The A-Y-P publicity department had been promoting Alaska's bounty to magazines and newspapers across the country. Only a small percentage of those who read these stories would travel to Alaska, but many more might venture as far as Seattle. The exposition publicity bureau offered free trips to the fair to the winners of contests sponsored by 208 newspapers in 35 states. Washington school children were encouraged to write to their Eastern counterparts about the exciting fair to come, and many Eastern newspapers picked up on this winsome campaign.

Though centered in Seattle, the A-Y-P Exposition was a statewide event. Every county in the state had appropriated funds to participate in the fair, and four counties — Yakima, King, Spokane, and Chehalis (now Grays Harbor County) — constructed buildings.

Many Washington cities formed Exposition Clubs to pull together displays that would promote the riches of their particular county. The Tacoma Chamber of Commerce sponsored a rail trip to Los Angeles to promote the fair. Stopping in more than 30 cities, the Washingtonians made speeches, shook hands, and affixed A-Y-P pins and booster buttons onto every available lapel. The train, noted the *Seattle Mail and Herald,* carried "hundreds of pounds of ammunition in the form of literature on the Exposition of 1909 and the State of Washington ... the 1909 fair is not to be considered as 'The Seattle Exposition.' It belongs to the entire Pacific Coast."

During October 1908, the massive logs that would be used by to erect the Forestry Building and also serve as decorative elements were felled near the Snohomish County town of Hazel.

Railroads promoted the fair with low excursion rates, advertised the fair nationwide, and subscribed to exposition stock. For three years prior to the fair, the Seattle City Council mentioned the exposition on every piece of promotional material and correspondence. The nation — even the world — could hardly fail to notice that they had been invited to attend the A-Y-P Exposition.

The Arctic Brotherhood was the first fraternal organization to break ground at the fair. In November 1908 members of the group gathered at the foundation of their building on the exposition grounds. With great ceremony a team of malamute dogs dragged the first log into place. Scheduled to house an exhibition of Northland artifacts and to be the Arctic Brotherhood's clubhouse during the fair, the building was given to the University of Washington after the fair for use by students from Alaska and the Yukon.

TELL YOUR FRIENDS

February 7, 1909, was Home Letter Day: everyone in Seattle was "expected" to write at least five letters to distant friends inviting them to come to the fair. Major social, professional, and fraternal organizations across the nation also received letters of invitation. Seattleites who belonged to national associations deluged their groups with promotional materials aimed at making Seattle the site for 1909 conventions. Many Seattle residents purchased formal printed invitations to mail to friends.

"A-Y-P — Only 79 days in which to clean up the city — A-Y-P" blared a rather desperate headline on March 14, 1909. The article exhorted — begged — Mr. Business Man, Mr. Property Owner, and Mrs. Housewife to throw their efforts into cleaning up the city.

Accompanying photographs documenting trash, debris, and refuse heaped on property throughout the city vividly reinforced the need for civic tidying. Nearly a month later the mayor was still pleading with Seattle citizens to deal with the mess. Streets near the university and exposition grounds were torn up for a paving project that floundered due to poor weather. Nearby homeowners who wanted to beautify their lawns were impeded by a three-quarter-mile-long heap of excavated dirt that snaked along the curb.

The district engineer hemmed and hawed, and University District residents sometimes awoke to find that during the night refuse had been dumped on nearby vacant lots. The Seattle Electric Company was feverishly laying new streetcar tracks, important work that nevertheless added to the chaos. "Excuses are already whispered around and some are made openly," warned *The Seattle Daily Times*. "No excuse will be accepted by the people who are watching the city and nothing but results should be considered."

FINAL TOUCHES

On April 23, a firm from Boston named H. A. Tower Company became the first exhibitor to complete installation in the Manufactures Building.

On May 19, Seattle celebrated the arrival of the pathfinder car as it completed the 4,000 mile journey from New York to the A-Y-P grounds to mark the path for the transcontinental automobile race that would begin on Opening Day.

Pay Streak concessionaires had to excavate their own sites, erect the structures that housed their concessions, and, in some cases, hire or transport the necessary performers. Four Pay Streak attractions (the Ferris Wheel, Land of the Midnight Sun, Gold Camps of the North, and San Marino Theater) were not ready for opening day. The Ferris Wheel's delay was due to an accident in the Illinois factory. Workers busily hammered away on the grandstand for fireworks displays located at the foot of the Pay Streak.

By spring, some, but not all, of the many souvenir stands were in place. These stands, designed to sell postcards, candy, chewing gum, and ice cream cones, were built off site, transported by wagon to the grounds, and positioned near exposition buildings. When one of these stands was planted in front of the Oregon Building, the building's superintendent, F. J. Smith, had it thrown into the street. Armed with a revolver, he swore that anyone who tried to replace it

would do so over his dead body. California Building staff chimed in that if any stand was placed near their building, they would dynamite it. These states had paid thousands of dollars to grade their sites and lay turf, and they did not want the grass marred by booths. Other states, including Washington, endorsed Oregon's position. Faced with potential mutiny, exposition officials backed down and promised to place sales booths only near state and county buildings that welcomed them. This did not stop exposition guards from bodily removing Idaho Building commissioner A. D. McKinlay from the grounds when he tried to stop a worker — who had threatened to hit him with a shovel — from digging a booth foundation on the Idaho Building lawn. Chilberg and Nadeau both offered McKinlay an apology.

One week before opening day, Seattle city engineer R. H. Thomson and Superintendent of Public Works A. V. Bouillon squabbled over whether or not dozens of contractors who had not yet finished their city improvement work should be granted extensions. Much of the street improvement work simply was not done. But new streetcar lines were up and running, prepared to carry carloads

TOP LEFT: Skilled plasterers pause to be photographed in front of their work; ABOVE: Model for the large wolf sculpture that (along with sculptures of a polar bear, an ox, and a mountain lion) adorned the Arctic Circle; OPPOSITE PAGE: Washingtonians sent promotional postcards and letters to friends across the country alerting them to the upcoming A-Y-P Exposition.

of fairgoers through city streets whether the sidewalks they rolled past were ready or not. On many streets, Seattle City Light installed ornamental streetlamps, each with a cluster of round globe-lamps.

University of Washington students and alumni snapped up summer fair jobs. Among the jobs held by these willing workers were guards, gatemen, rickshaw pullers, Pay Streak barkers, publicity department staff, works department staff, athletic department staff, and newspaper correspondents. Two-hundred college men from schools around the country arrived to fill other jobs, blacking boots, waiting tables, selling view books, and hawking peanuts to cover their fall tuition. New hotels, from the palatial Sorrento overlooking Elliott Bay to the practical Ye College Inn, steps away from the exposition's main gate, opened their doors and braced for the throngs of people that would soon have bellboys hopping. Households throughout the region readied their homes for visiting friends and relatives, and many Seattleites planned to rent their guestrooms to fair-going strangers. Sixty-five conventions were scheduled for Seattle during the course of the fair, and more groups were expected to join them.

OVERTURE

On Sunday, May 23, 18,648 people paid to enter the fairgrounds. They were not permitted into any building or Pay Streak attraction, but they stared through the fence at Igorrote villagers (members of a Filipino tribe to be part of an exhibition), strolled clean exposition boulevards watching workers bustling about, and visited the live game exhibit area. On May 27 the grounds were closed to the public so that exhibitors could ready their booths. This was no simple task, and three days later the *Seattle Post-Intelligencer* printed a long list detailing which booths (including Shredded Wheat, Heinz Pickles, most of the county booths in the Manufactures Building, and many more) were not yet ready. Booths ready by Wednesday (National Cash Register, Welch Grape Juice, Asotin County, and others) received awards.

Army and Navy personnel asked for a gate where uniformed military personnel could get in free, but exposition officials declined to provide one. Meanwhile money changers and turnstile operators rehearsed their jobs using real money at a special practice turnstile set up in the Auditorium Building.

A-Y-P guards and turnstile operators ready for crowds at the Main Gate.

With two days until opening, John C. Olmsted strolled through the grounds he had designed. Olmsted called the fair's natural vistas — Mount Rainier, the Olympic and Cascade mountain ranges, Lake Union, and Lake Washington — its best feature.

On May 29 the Seattle Parks Commission finished final work on the university extension of Washington Park Boulevard, giving fairgoers arriving by automobile a graceful connection between Washington Park Boulevard and the A-Y-P south entrance.

On May 31 the University of Washington held commencement exercises in the Manufactures Building. The Government and King County buildings hosted receptions, giving VIPs and other invited guests a thrilling preview of the next day's excitement.

Washington caught its collective breath. "The World's Fair That Will Be Ready" was ready to begin.

JUNE 1909

THE ALASKA-YUKON-PACIFIC EXPOSITION OPENS TO GREAT POPULAR ANTICIPATION RIGHT ON SCHEDULE ON JUNE 1, 1909. PRESIDENT TAFT PRESSES A NUGGET-ENCRUSTED TELEGRAPH KEY IN WASHINGTON, D.C., TRIGGERING A BOOMING VOLLEY OF CANNON FIRE OVER LAKE UNION. IN NEW YORK, FIVE AUTOS FIRE UP FOR A RACE TO THE A-Y-P. AMONG THOSE TAKING IT ALL IN ARE OFFICERS OF THE IMPERIAL JAPANESE NAVY, WHOSE CRUISERS *ASO* AND *SOYA* ARE ANCHORED OFF SEATTLE.

THE GATES OF THE ALASKA-YUKON-Pacific Exposition opened promptly at 8:30 on the morning of Tuesday, June 1, 1909. The skies were cloudy, but that didn't bother the thousands of people already lined up. Many held season passes, which had sold out before the fair opened.

Streetcars operated by the Seattle Electric Company pulled up to the gates almost continuously. Streetcars from downtown ran along the Eastlake route at a rate of one every 30 seconds. The Wallingford line arrived once a minute, and the Madrona and Broadway runs pulled in every five minutes.

There were 42 coin-operated turnstiles at the gates, each operated by a guard. Only one turnstile was designated for use by those with passes. The eccentric Robert Patten, known as the "Umbrella Man," showed up in his umbrella hat carrying Season Pass No. 13. Fourteen-year-old Al Rochester, whose mother represented Washington in a singing competition at the 1893 World's Columbian Exposition, flashed his pass, and ran to his job operating a bread-slicer at one of the concession stands on the Pay Streak. The concession lasted all of two days, but Al, as an employee, got a free pass to the fair and attended almost every day that summer.

This turnstile was also used by exposition officials such as Henry Broderick — at 29, the youngest A-Y-P trustee. Broderick was prominent in real estate, and was instrumental in acquiring property for

ABOVE: Opening Day pass; OPPOSITE PAGE: Opening Day crowds filled the A-Y-P Natural Amphitheatre to overflowing.

the Union Pacific Railroad. Washington Equal Suffrage Association President Emma Smith DeVoe paid 50 cents to get in, as did Seattle Socialist leader Dr. Herman F. Titus. Mary Brown of Tacoma, state superintendent of the Woman's Christian Temperance Union, showed up at the gates with her cohorts, ready to patrol the grounds and guard young women from mashers and ne'er-do-wells.

When Seattle Chief of Police Irving Ward arrived in full dress uniform, one gatekeeper didn't recognize him and refused to allow him in. Ward sputtered, and told him that as police chief, he didn't have to pay to get in. The gatekeeper stood firm until Ward threatened to arrest him, at which point he backed down and let the chief in, free of charge. Since the turnstiles were coin-operated, Ward had to jump the gate.

Edmund A. Smith had looked forward to opening day, and to showing off the invention that made him wealthy. Six years earlier, Smith had patented a machine that could clean salmon 55 times faster than could human workers. Since many Northwest cannery workers were Chinese immigrants, Smith unabashedly named his invention the "Iron Chink," and it revolutionized the canning industry. The machine was on display at the A-Y-P., but Smith never got there. On his way to the fair, the gasoline tank on his car exploded and he died in the fire.

Exhibit buildings and amusements along the Pay Streak were told to stay closed until after the noon opening ceremonies. Most people wandered around enjoying the architecture, but some made their way into the Spokane Building. Spokane officials claimed "they couldn't help it," and opened their doors ahead of time to ease the pressure of the waiting crowd.

At 9:30, a military parade began at the southernmost end of the fairgrounds leading towards Geyser Basin, the pool and high-spouting fountain around which the main buildings, called the Court of Honor, were arranged. At this focal point of the fair, high officers reviewed members of the United States Army and Navy and also of the Imperial Japanese Navy, which had been invited to participate.

Official numbered daily tickets to the fair.

FREQUENTLY ASKED QUESTIONS

The main telephone number for the fair was A-Y-P 1909. Operators stood by to connect callers directly to each building's telephone.

The grounds were open from 8 a.m. until midnight. The main exhibits closed at 5 p.m. but Pay Streak attractions were open until midnight.

Admission to the grounds cost 50 cents, 25 cents for children 6 to 12, and free for younger children. After 6 p.m. admission was reduced to 25 cents.

Fairgoers were instructed to deposit either pre-purchased admission tickets or exact change into boxes by the turnstiles, or to show a pass. Turnstiles were segregated by payment type, and pass turnstiles were open around the clock so that those working and living on the grounds could come and go. Baby carriages could pass through special gates at each end of the row of turnstiles.

Two parking garages, one near the south gate and one on lower 15th Avenue, accommodated automobiles for 25 cents an hour.

Rolling wicker chairs with a guide to push them could be rented for 75 cents an hour. Rickshaws with pullers could also be hired.

Infant care was available in the Woman's Building and as part of the Baby Incubator Exhibit concession.

A branch of the post office could be found in the Government Building and a telegraph office in the King County Building.

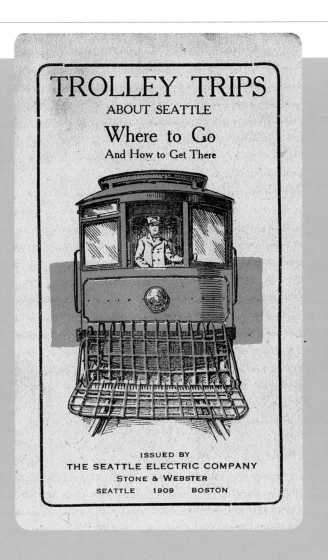

TROLLEY TRIPS

ABOUT SEATTLE

Where to Go

And How to Get There

ISSUED BY
THE SEATTLE ELECTRIC COMPANY
STONE & WEBSTER
SEATTLE   1909   BOSTON

GETTING THERE

By car and by horse-drawn carriage, many fairgoers took newly improved direct routes: Westlake to Denny Way to Eastlake and via the newly widened Latona Bridge over Lake Union; Pike Street to Broadway to 10th Avenue N to the Latona Bridge; Interlaken Drive around the end of Union Bay. By streetcar: via the Eastlake, Wallingford, Madrona Park, or 23rd Avenue routes. By steamers on Lake Washington: from Madison, Leschi, and Madrona parks to the A-Y-P Exposition's water landing. These embarkation points were reached from downtown via the Madison Street and Yesler Way cable lines and the Madrona electric line. The Latona Bridge (1891–1919) crossed Lake Union at the future location of the Ship Canal Bridge. Fairgoers also arrived by bicycle and, of course, by foot.

Exposition promoters were proud to have officers and sailors of the Japanese Navy in attendance. Days before, folks in downtown Seattle marveled at the two fighting ships — the *Aso* and *Soya* — moored in Elliott Bay. Both vessels were Russian cruisers salvaged by Japan after the Russo-Japanese War, whose conclusion in 1905 had been mediated by the United States. The *Soya* had been built in Philadelphia.

After the military parade, the crowd moved next to the amphitheatre for opening ceremonies. Patriotic music spilled out over the crowd. After an invocation and opening speeches, railroad magnate James J. Hill delivered the keynote address. Hill noted that until very recently the Pacific Northwest had been considered remote and isolated from the rest of the nation. He described the two events that were primarily responsible for its subsequent growth and development: the transcontinental railroad and the discovery of great riches in Alaska. But rather than look back at past accomplishments, Hill commended Northwesterners for their spirit of progress, and termed the exposition "The Fair that Faces Forward."

BELOW: Michigan State Society members raised money for their own clubhouse building at the fair; **LEFT:** Many visiting fairgoers also enjoyed the region's other attractions.

IT OFFICIALLY BEGINS

Promptly at noon, fair President John Chilberg announced that he was about to notify President Taft, who stood at the ready in the East Room of the White House, that the fair could begin. Taft would officially open the fair by pressing a telegraph key encrusted with nuggets from the mine of George Carmack, whose discovery had started the Klondike Gold Rush. As the audience waited for Taft to press the key, a telegram from the president was read aloud.

Bishop Frederick W. Keator read the benediction, and just as he was about to finish, Taft's signal came through. Cannons fired at the lakefront, and a large gong at the back of the platform rang out. All eyes looked up at a gigantic flag that had been close-furled between two large fir trees behind the stage.

The flag unfurled, and the crowd erupted with cheers. Hundreds of high-school students sitting in reserved seats in the front row pulled out small flags they had been told to conceal and began to wave them wildly while singing "America." After they finished singing, the crowd cheered for more than five minutes.

Meanwhile, another historic event was taking place back east. At the same moment that President Taft pressed the golden key in the White House, five automobiles in New York started their engines for a transcontinental race across America. A sixth car left New York a few days later.

One month earlier, a pathfinder car had made its way across the country, looking for the best route for the Itala, Shawmut, Acme, Stearns, and two Model T Fords that were entered in the race. Traveling the eastern half of the United States would be relatively easy, as there were plenty of roads. But the road-poor Rocky Mountains guaranteed that the latter stages of the race would be a grind.

After the opening ceremonies, the crowds dispersed to take in the sights, while the dignitaries attended a luncheon at the New York State Building. Originally, the luncheon was scheduled to be held at the Washington State Building. However, a majority of state commissioners disallowed the event, insisting that the building should be open to the public at all times, and not closed for a certain few. Governor Marion E. Hay and other officials were upset that New York had to act as host for Washington's fair, but grumblingly abided by the decision. Most dignitaries who visited A-Y-P were feted in the New York Building.

OPENING DAY JITTERS

Many folks were hoping to see the dirigible "A-Y-P" take to the air, and close to 3,000 people gathered near the stadium at 3 p.m. to witness its launch, but pilot James C. "Bud" Mars, who won first prize with the airship at the 1907 International Race in St. Louis, couldn't get the gasoline engine to start. Disappointed, the crowd wandered off to see what else the fair had to offer.

Another mishap occurred when 3-year-old Beatrice Bergeron of Seattle fell into the Geyser Basin, where she had dropped her rubber ball. This happened out of sight of the girl's mother, who was transfixed by one of the concert bands. Fortunately, Walter Hendrickson of Walla Walla happened to see the child fall, and dove into the pond to save her.

Exposition officials were astonished that there were no reports of robbery or pickpocket activity on opening day. There was only one arrest, when A-Y-P Exposition Chief of Police Charles Wappenstein pinched a huckster who was trying to sell bogus stock in the exposition airship. The biggest task that exposition police dealt with was reuniting lost children with their parents.

At 8 p.m. in the Auditorium Building, the Schubert Club held a concert featuring the noted Russian baritone, Albert Janpolski. At the moment the first song ended, all the lights in the building went

The A-Y-P airship floats dramatically over Geyser Basin.

AIRSHIP A.Y.P.E. OVER GEYSER BASIN

The rainfall also doused the fireworks show that had been planned as the day's crowning finale.

Attendance on the first day was close to 80,000 people, and officials stated that it would have been higher had the weather been more agreeable. The next day, attendance came to 17,000, which exceeded expectations.

BROTHERS IN ARMS

On June 2, ceremonies honoring Bering Sea Day were abandoned because most of the Alaska fishermen had visited the fair the day before and many were home packing for the first sailings of fishing season. But prominent guests from all over Alaska and the Yukon Territory were on hand for the dedication of the Arctic Brotherhood Building.

The Arctic Brotherhood was a fraternal order of Klondike gold miners founded on board the S.S. *City of Seattle* in 1899 while en route to Skagway, the Alaska gateway to the Klondike. Their building at the A-Y-P was an impressive log structure, akin to a lodge. After the dedication, they immediately donated it to the trustees and regents of the University of Washington for whatever use the university saw fit after the fair was over.

Bud Mars finally got his airship up in the sky on Wednesday evening. On Thursday evening he gashed his wrist on a cogwheel while in flight. He landed safely, but his bandages may have hindered his movement the next day, when he briefly lost control of the dirigible and almost dunked it into Lake Union. Fortunately, he steered it onto a barge, narrowly escaping a cold plunge.

Military might was on display for most of the first week, with athletic events held between the United States Army and Navy, and a special day in honor of the Japanese Navy, which had a keen interest in the war exhibits housed in the Government Building. Many of the Japanese sailors were seen taking frequent notes on the military displays and demonstrations.

out. After spending 15 minutes in the dark, the choir quietly sang "My Country 'Tis of Thee" until it was announced that the concert would be rescheduled for later in the week. The audience slowly exited the darkened building, only to discover that it was pouring rain.

To escape the deluge, almost everyone on the fairgrounds made a mad scramble to the exits. The first bottleneck came at the turnstiles, and the second came at the streetcar terminals. The Seattle Electric Company had scheduled cars to arrive regularly, but they weren't prepared for tens of thousand of people to leave en masse.

Some people leaving the fairgrounds got a shocking experience when they crossed the lawn in front of the King County Building: A nearby power wire had become grounded because of the heavy rain, and current flowed through the soaked earth, effectively electrifying the grass. The power was shut off to all buildings around the Arctic Circle until the defective wire could be found. The short caused a small fire inside the south wall of the King County Building, but it was extinguished before it could do much harm.

THIS PAGE: Japanese Rear Admiral Hikojiro Ijichi visited the fair on opening day; OPPOSITE PAGE: Young fairgoers pause near the Geyser Basin on Children's Day, June 5, 1909.

PRECEDING SPREAD: The fair's most majestic built features were the Court of Honor buildings and Cascade Fountain. Fairgoers resting near the fountain could enjoy a view of Mt. Rainier.

ABOVE LEFT: The Fairy Gorge Tickler provided thrills by jostling riders against each other as they careened down a twisting track; **ABOVE RIGHT:** Many exhibits in the United States Government Building stressed the country's military prowess; **BELOW:** Children's Day pin-back button.

KIDS, YOUNG AND OLD

Many adults took in the sights on the weekdays, but when the fair's first Saturday rolled around, it was time for the youngsters to have fun. June 5 was Children's Day, and crowds of kids filled the fairgrounds. More than 1,000 boys and girls came over from Kitsap County, filling the ferryboats that crossed Puget Sound. Total attendance that day surpassed 40,000.

At the Natural Amphitheatre, a chorus of 1,700 children sang patriotic songs played by the official A-Y-P band. The Japanese naval band also played, and the youngsters sang Japan's national anthem, which they had learned in English weeks before. Their voices sang out, "May the Mikado's empire stand, till a thousand, yes, ten thousand years shall roll."

Frank Cooper, superintendent of Seattle schools, gave a short speech about hard work and dedication, and at the end of the program each of the children donned a red, white or blue apron, filling the stage with an immense human flag .

With the formal ceremonies complete, the children explored the exposition. Many parents took their sons and daughters to see the educational exhibits, but most wanted to take in the amusements on the Pay Streak. More than 11,000 tickets were sold at the Fairy Gorge Tickler, a ride that featured cars on wheels that rolled down a hill, guided by rails on a twisty path. The Tickler broke the record for number of passengers on a ride in one day at any exposition.

That night, the big fireworks show that was supposed to have taken place on opening day was held at the foot of the Pay Streak. Seventy-nine different aerial bombs and ground displays were ignited, including gigantic fire portraits of James J. Hill and John Chilberg.

BY WEEK'S END

Chilberg's days were busy. In the morning he usually attended to business at the Scandinavian-American Bank, and then headed to the fairgrounds at around 11 a.m. If there were any important guests that day, he made sure to meet them. If a special luncheon was being held, he attended. Then it was off to the Administration Building to handle exposition business until 6, after which he might attend a banquet. In the evenings, he personally inspected the grounds, making sure that everyone's needs were attended to. He returned home late, and then got up early the next morning to do it all over again.

On Sundays, the A-Y-P was open shorter hours, between 1 and 11 p.m., and admission was half-price. Many families brought picnic lunches to eat in the noonday sun. Attendance on the first Sunday, June 6, came to more than 20,000, and those who wandered around marveled at how far Seattle had come since the Great Fire, which

Visitors arriving through the main entrance at NE 40th Street and 15th Avenue NE were greeted by Lorado Taft's George Washington statue.

SUNDAY OPENINGS

The question of whether an exposition should welcome visitors on Sundays dogged all American fairs during the early years of the twentieth century. If the traditional Christian religious convention that Sunday was a day for restful spiritual reflection held true, educating and amusing oneself at the fair was at best a gaffe and at worst a sin. Federal appropriations for expositions usually stipulated Sunday closures, although for some reason the A-Y-P's appropriation did not.

A-Y-P Exposition officials decided to open the gates on Sunday, but not until 1 p.m. — after potential fairgoers would presumably have already attended Sunday morning church services. Sunday was the only day many workers had leisure, so this compromise removed the need to choose between piety and pleasure. Those more familiar with the saloon rail than the communion rail benefited from Sunday openings as well, since saloons in Seattle were closed that day. In the end the United States government buildings were closed on Sundays, but other attractions were open. Pay Streak attractions could operate, but their ballyhoo men were not allowed to spiel. An average of 25,000 people attended the fair each Sunday.

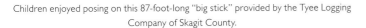

Children enjoyed posing on this 87-foot-long "big stick" provided by the Tyee Logging Company of Skagit County.

had destroyed much of the city's business district exactly 20 years ago that day.

The A-Y-P Exposition was less than a week old, and by all accounts it was a huge success. The Seattle Post Office reported that hundreds of thousands of Alaska-Yukon-Pacific stamps had been sold, and that countless A-Y-P postcards were being sent all over the country. Motion pictures of the fair were shown at the Orpheum before being sent back east as advertisements.

MORE MISHAPS

Misfortune struck on June 7, when Alaska, one of the horses at the A-Y-P fire house, had to be destroyed. During the morning drill, the big bay horse stepped into the spokes of a wheel, shattering its leg. Faithful until the end, the steed continued forward, hobbled into position, and waited for the snap of the harness, ready to move out.

When the firefighters realized what had happened, and saw the perseverance of their good friend, many of them broke down and cried. "Oh, Alaska," sobbed one of the men, while clinging to the horse's neck. Nothing could be done to ease the animal's pain and it had to be shot.

The fire crew had little time to grieve. Later that day a blaze started in the woods near the south fence, most likely from a cigarette butt flicked from the soldiers' camp. The blaze came perilously close to igniting a large cache of fireworks stored nearby for the nightly displays, but it was put out after five hours.

The day was jinxed. In the morning, a perambulator carrying an Igorrote baby escaped its guardian's grip, rolled down an asphalt walk, and tipped over. Fortunately, the baby landed safely in a bed of flowers. That afternoon a woman fell down the spiral stairway in the Forestry Building and broke her collarbone. Closer to nightfall, one of the walkways became electrified when wires short-circuited beneath it. A man and his son doubled over in pain, but were able to roll onto the grass before any grievous injury occurred.

HAWAIIANS, HOO-HOOS, AND HOLY SISTERS

Things got off to a better start the next day when the Hawaii Building finally opened its doors. This exhibit had been delayed due to a late arrival aboard the United States transport *Dix*, and Hawaiian commissioners had spent the last few days feverishly readying the display. Once inside, visitors gazed at 40-foot canoes made out of koa wood, a big pyramid of coconuts, and a giant 30-foot-tall pineapple composed of smaller pineapples. Exhibitors had problems with the Hawaiian sugar palace (a model of the Hawaiian royal palace crafted in brown sugar) as passersby kept snapping off parts of the structure to eat, and children surreptitiously licked away most of the sugar.

Visitors to the fairgrounds also got to see some new exhibits in other buildings. The old Territorial Seal hammered out by an Olympia blacksmith 56 years earlier was installed in the Forestry Building. In back of the Government Building, a 55-ton steel railroad car, used to carry mail, had been set up over the weekend under the watchful eye of postal officials.

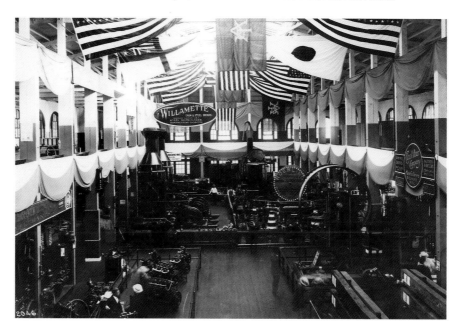

BELOW: Items displayed in the Machinery Building were required to be functional, practical, and relative to "Western Lifestyle"; TOP RIGHT: Brass disc used in the Hoo-Hoo House.

When J. C. "Bud" Mars took to the air in his A-Y-P dirigible, his wife lent moral support from the ground.

June 9 was Grocers' Day, and just about every grocery store in Seattle was closed so that owners and workers could visit the fair. Also that day, a wedding was held at the Hoo-Hoo House, home to the fraternal order of forestry workers. Since mystic Hoo-Hoo symbols included black cats and the number 9, the ceremony was attended by 99 people, and Bandersnatch, one of the nine Hoo-Hoo House cats, rested at the feet of the clergyman during the service.

When Sydney Smith and Birdie Ahstrom were declared husband and wife, a great Hoo-Hoo yell was given, scaring Bandersnatch out of the room. This was considered a good omen by the Hoo-Hoo brethren, who also offered up nine witnesses to sign the marriage document.

On June 10, Bud Mars suffered another airship mishap. This time the gasbag started leaking at 500 feet in the air, causing a rapid

TOP: Wenatchee Valley residents proudly displayed their big red apples; **BOTTOM:** The North Yakima Juvenile Band traveled to the fair to perform on Yakima Day.

descent. The dirigible landed hard in the stadium, smashing its rudder and cracking one of the propellers. Within a few hours, Mars and his crew made repairs and the craft was ready to fly again.

Touring the fairgrounds that day was Mother Francesca Xavier Cabrini, head of the Missionary Sisters of the Sacred Heart. She spent much of her time in the Manufactures Building, inspecting an exhibit of embroidery, needlework, and paintings created by orphans from Seattle's Mount Carmel Mission, which Mother Cabrini had established in 1903.

APPLES AND LEMONADE

Early on June 11, guards thought they saw smoke coming from the roof of the Agriculture Building, but when firefighters arrived they discovered that it was only a giant cloud of gnats. Later that day, swarms of visitors — including a special train carrying more than 300 people — came from Eastern Washington to take part in Yakima County Day. Farmers boasted over their mouth-watering apples, each staking a claim to where the best were grown.

One Yakima resident signed the register in the Yakima County building claiming that his town beat out Wenatchee as home of the Washington apple. A Wenatchee girl disagreed, stating that their apples were larger. A thirsty visitor from Minnesota stayed out of the fray, and pined for a nearby saloon, maybe for even a glass of hard cider. "Lead me to an oasis in this land of pop and lemonade," he wrote.

But most folks liked a cool drink of lemonade during those warms days, and many of them enjoyed their quaffs on the porch of the Washington State Building.

Easy chairs were available there, and one could often catch someone taking a short snooze after a long day's hike. The local papers also recommended that visitors rest now and then to ward off "A-Y-P headache," and suggested "smoked eyeglasses" to fend off the bright sunshine.

LEFT: Wenatchee pin-back booster button; **TOP RIGHT:** French waffles and root beer were menu items at this refreshment booth near the Igorrote Village; **BOTTOM RIGHT:** A giant lemon made of lemons amused California Building visitors.

GEORGE WASHINGTON STATUE

The George Washington statue has been a prominent fixture on the University of Washington campus since its unveiling on Flag Day, 1909. Sculpted by Lorado Taft and presented to the university by the Rainier Chapter of the Daughters of the American Revolution (D.A.R.), the statue was funded with help from the Washington State Legislature, along with donations from children around the state.

After the fair, it remained on a temporary base for some time due to a lack of funds for a new pedestal. In the 1930s, the Works Progress Administration built a tall stone base, which was dedicated on June 14, 1939, exactly 30 years after the statue's unveiling. The George Washington statue now stands a block north of its original location, and on each Presidents' Day, the D.A.R. lays flowers at its base.

FLAG AND FOREFATHER

Flag Day was celebrated with patriotic zeal. The giant flagpole, located east of the Government Building, was formally presented to the University of Washington by the Sons of the American Revolution and the Page Lumber Company. Almost 200 feet high, the Washington fir was cut in Pierce County and five railroad flatcars were required to transport it to the fairgrounds.

But the day's big event was the unveiling of the George Washington statue, sculpted by Lorado Taft. French Ambassador Jules Jusserand was on hand for the event, as were delegates from the Daughters of the American Revolution, which commissioned the statue. The sculpture was located near the main gates, but plans were made to move it elsewhere on campus after the fair.

Formal ceremonies were held in the auditorium. Jusserand and others gave speeches, but when it came time for Washington Governor Marion Hay to approach the stage, he was nowhere to be found. As it turned out, he thought that the ceremonies were going to be held outside, and he waited near the statue for over an hour, expecting crowds to show up. Eventually, they did, after all the speeches were finished.

At the unveiling, the strings to remove the flag draped around George Washington were pulled by 4-year-old Eleanor Washington Caldwell. Born in Seattle, the little girl was the great-grandniece of America's first president.

HEADS OF STATES

Governor Hay was only one of four Western governors to visit the fair that week. On June 15, Idaho Governor James H. Brady inspected the fairgrounds, but mostly stayed close to the Idaho Building to meet with visitors.

Meanwhile a delegation from the California promotion committee had arrived in Seattle. A trainload of more than 100 men representing commercial interests in California were ready to meet with like-minded individuals from Washington to further cement friendly relations between the states. With them was California Governor James Gillett, along with members of his staff and family.

The Californians and Washingtonians enjoyed a grand banquet at the New York State Building on the night of June 16. They had hoped to be joined by Governor Frank Benson of Oregon, but his

Visitors from Los Angeles pose for a photograph at the fair's water entrance on Lake Washington.

train did not arrive until the next day. On Friday, June 18, Benson formally dedicated the Oregon Building.

That same day, Washington State Fisheries Superintendent Perry Baker was given a baby seal that had been caught near South Bend and brought to the fair by the executive commissioner of Pacific County. The young pup enjoyed warm milk from a baby bottle, and once she was accustomed to her new home, followed Baker around like a puppy dog.

As delegates tried to figure out how to set up a tank for their new aquatic pet, things got really wet on the other side of the fairgrounds when a city water main burst right next to the main gates. The man in the money-changing booth noticed water seeping up through the asphalt. He quickly grabbed the change box and ran, just before a geyser erupted out of the ground. Smaller spouts popped up nearby, undermining most of the pavement. Workers immediately began repairing the damage.

62

MAINTAINING ORDER

Some joked that the money-changer probably ran thinking that criminals were tunneling up into the booth to steal the cashbox. In fact, crime at the fair was minimal. Not a single pickpocketing was reported until well into June. The victim was an embarrassed Tacoma police officer who sheepishly explained that a thief had pinched his badge, which he had put in his pocket, along with four silver dollars.

Some thieves may have been deterred by Chief Wappenstein's comments to the press. Earlier in the month he informed the papers that his A-Y-P cops planned to "beat and maul" any thieves they caught. He also commented that pickpockets would get the treatment from "big-fisted guards wearing hob-nailed shoes."

Wappenstein maintained tight discipline among his guards. A few weeks into the fair two were fired for drinking on the job. Days later, the body of one of them was found floating in Elliott Bay, whether by accident or suicide is not known. He was last seen alive, intoxicated, in Pioneer Square.

Overall, the guards at the fair had an easy time. Pinkerton agents who had worked as guards at other fairs noted that the absence of liquor at the A-Y-P meant almost no rowdyism.

CASH AND DASH

On June 19, an impressive display was installed in the center of the Alaska Building. More than $500,000 of gold dust, nuggets, and bars glittered inside a heavily fortified case surrounded by steel and glass. A few days later, the Scandinavian-American Bank added to the pile, bringing its worth to more than $1 million.

RIGHT: A-Y-P police chief Charles Wappenstein meted out severe penalties for even minor infractions;
OPPOSITE PAGE: Ford Model T driver Bert Scott and mechanic C. J. Smith captured first prize in the highly publicized transcontinental auto race, June 23, 1909. Henry Ford, far right; Robert Guggenheim, center, leaning on car.

On Monday, June 21, the Utah Building opened its doors for the first time, and on the next day, the Michigan Club Building opened. When the fair was being planned, it was hoped that Michigan would have its own building at the fair, but officials in the Wolverine State failed to appropriate money for it. Local Michigan natives raised the money themselves, and built a smaller structure for their headquarters.

The new buildings got lots of buzz, but the big excitement that week was the completion of the cross-country road race that began in New York on the day that the fair opened. No one was more excited than Robert Guggenheim, the race promoter, who recently had been arrested in Seattle for driving his own high-powered car down city streets at an estimated 60 miles an hour.

FIRST IN A FORD

News reports kept fairgoers informed about the race. In Wyoming, the Shawmut was in the lead. In Idaho, Ford No. 1 was ahead. Ford Car No. 2 was the first racer to enter Washington. By the time Ford Car No. 2 crossed Snoqualmie Pass, it was hours ahead of the second place Shawmut. At 12:30 p.m., on June 24, Ford Car No. 2 reached the fairgrounds, and broke a red silk tape at the main gate. Its drivers were covered in dust and mud.

More than 10,000 people were on hand to witness the end of the race, including hundreds of Civil War veterans celebrating State Grand Army of the Republic Day. The Model T was driven to the stadium, where it made five exhibition laps. A place of honor was assigned to the car in the Mines Building, but when the racers drove it up the front steps, they discovered that the doorway wasn't wide enough. They drove it back down and around the building to a separate entryway.

Henry Ford, president of Ford Motor Company and owner of the winning car, was on hand to share in the triumph, and he couldn't have been happier. The 46-year-old businessman had introduced the Model T only a

THE IGORROTES

Exhibitions of indigenous peoples were common, expected features at world expositions during the late nineteenth and early twentieth centuries. Presented as anthropological and ethnological educational exhibits, these "living displays" of men, women, and children — oftentimes in a faux "natural" environment — emphasized cultural differences between European and non-European peoples by portraying certain ethnic groups as inferior and uncivilized.

One such display at the A-Y-P — the Igorrote Village — provided fairgoers with a skewed view of Filipino life. This exhibit was markedly smaller than similar ones shown at other fairs. More than 1,200 Filipinos were exhibited at the 1904 Louisiana Purchase Exposition in St. Louis in contrast to a few dozen individuals who populated the Igorrote Village at the A-Y-P.

The Igorrotes trace their roots from the Central Cordillera Mountains of Northern Luzon, Philippines. When Spanish soldiers failed to subjugate these mountain people during Spain's occupation of the Philippines in the 1500s, the Spaniards launched a war of words against the Igorrotes, referring to them as primitive savages and headhunters. Centuries later, after America occupied the Philippines following the 1898 Spanish-American War, pro-imperialist factions in the United States reinforced these stereotypes in a propaganda campaign of their own.

To convince the American public that the Philippine Islands needed American intervention in order to become more "civilized," newspapers throughout the United States depicted Filipinos as racially inferior and incapable of self-governance. Igorrotes and other Filipino tribes were brought to America and exploited at a series of expositions, including the A-Y-P. Publicists described the Igorrotes as wild, untamed, savage, or barbaric.

Besides reinforcing stereotypes of Filipino inferiority, the exhibition of Igorrotes also provided sensationalism in an era of staid and upright social mores. The tribesmen were semi-nude — wearing what newspapers described as "gee-strings" — and many visitors expressed shock that the Igorrote sometimes ate dog, although it was a common practice in many cultures. Even the Lewis and Clark expedition, iconic purveyors of Western expansion, included dog meat in their diet.

These caricatures of the Igorrotes have lasted up until the present time, and have caused much shame and embarrassment to the Igorrote people, to the point where some members prefer not to be identified as "Igorot" (now the preferred spelling). Because of the negative connotations instilled by centuries of racism, the Igorot Global Organization was formed in 1995 to preserve the heritage and maintain the ethnic identity of this much-maligned group of people.

**LEFT: Igorrote men perform a ceremonial dance while children play in the dance circle and women gather on the sidelines;
CENTER INSET: Two Igorrote boys play on the Pay Streak;
RIGHT: The Robert M. Guggenheim Transcontinental Trophy was adorned with figureheads of Chief Seattle and with pictures of the Agricultural Building.**

few months earlier, and he was hoping his new automobile would catch on with the American public. It did.

Sixteen hours after the Model T was awarded the Guggenheim Trophy, the Shawmut arrived. Almost immediately, the drivers of the second-place car filed formal charges against Ford Car No. 2, claiming that its drivers had broken the rules. Five specific infractions were noted, the most grievous of which was that the drivers had replaced an axle during the race, which was expressly forbidden.

Robert Guggenheim took the complaints under consideration, but awarded the trophy and $2,055 prize to the Ford anyway. A suit was filed and a few months later the courts declared the Shawmut the winner. It didn't matter much to Henry Ford. The Model T's "victory" had already given Ford all the publicity he needed.

On Sunday, June 28, the Seattle Symphony moved its free weekend concerts from the auditorium into the Forestry Building. The Ferris Wheel finally opened on the Pay Streak. More people flocked to the fairgrounds, enjoying summer weather.

By the end of June 670,389 people had visited the A-Y-P Exposition — an average of 22,346 fairgoers each day.

A PAY·STREAK·SCENE.

JULY 1909

SUFFRAGISTS USE THE FAIR'S FULL PUBLIC RELATIONS POTENTIAL ON WOMAN SUFFRAGE DAY, MAKING THEIR CASE FOR WHY WOMEN SHOULD HAVE THE VOTE. THE DISPLAY OF IGORROTE VILLAGERS FROM THE PHILIPPINES DRAWS INTEREST, OPPROBRIUM, AND OFFICIAL BUNGLING. AND JAMES C. "BUD" MARS CONTINUES TO ALTERNATELY ENTERTAIN AND DISMAY THE CROWDS WITH HIS WAYWARD POWERED DIRIGIBLE. SWEDISH DAY PROVES A HIT, DESPITE THE ABSENCE OF A KEY GUEST. THE PACKED FAIRGROUNDS CONTINUE TO BE A LARGELY CRIME-FREE ZONE.

"I LIKE MY PORTLAND, BUT OH YOU SEATTLE!" crowed a dozen Oregon girls visiting the fair with a group sponsored by the *Portland Evening Telegram*.

Thousands of conventioneers, town delegations, VIPs, and other fairgoers arrived in Seattle via specially designated train cars or on their own private rail cars. All during the summer of 1909, 10 to 20 of these private cars and A-Y-P Specials were parked on the Northern Pacific Railway tracks west of King Street Station. Among the Specials arriving in early July were those carrying delegates from

the Epworth League — a Methodist youth organization — the Suffrage Special carrying more than 250 national leaders of the American suffrage movement, and an entire trainload of Hoboken, New Jersey, Elks who swung by the A-Y-P after attending their national convention in Los Angeles.

CHERRIES, ROSES, AND BURLY MEN

Thursday, July 1, was a great day for cherry-loving fairgoers — several tons of the delicious fruit were given away, 200,000 cherries from The Dalles Commercial Club's display in the Oregon Building alone. To mark A-Y-P Cherry Day, fruit growers in Washington, Utah, and Idaho also distributed their choicest cherries from booths throughout the Agriculture Building.

ABOVE RIGHT: The Elk's Circus special-day program predicted uproarious hilarity; OPPOSITE PAGE: Fairgoers pack the Pay Streak, A-Y-P's wildly popular midway.

Yakima County's booth spelled out "A-Y-P-E" in Royal Ann and Bing cherries. Visitors to the Idaho Building were treated to free cherry punch.

The following day, the women of Skagit County distributed free roses at the Woman's Building. The state Legislature was also in a giving mood, authorizing the A-Y-P commissioners to spend up to $10,000 to entertain official representatives of other states. And not to be outdone, A-Y-P officials gave the Igorrote villagers 50 brightly colored cotton "gee-strings."

July 3 was designated as Railway Men Day, King County Day, Coal Miners' Day, and Lumbermen and Loggers' Day. Festivities began with a parade featuring floats created by Seattle businesses. The rather long route took the marchers, floats, automobiles, and

Ezra Meeker's ox-drawn prairie schooner from Pioneer Place through downtown Seattle, north on Broadway, and on to the fair gate where waiting loggers, lumbermen, coal miners, and railway men joined the party. The railway men hosted the public wedding of a bride and groom named Margaret Anna Hall and C. A. Bebee at the foot of the Pay Streak and also tossed checks for varying amounts out of the A-Y-P dirigible.

HEY, BUD

Once again, Bud Mars's airship provided its own unexpected drama when it dropped abruptly into a tree near the Swedish Building. Mars's long-suffering wife pushed through 5,000 gawkers to assist her husband from the wreckage. Meanwhile a cornet player in

Flowerbeds embrace the Arctic Circle. Court of Honor buildings visible (from far left): European/Foreign Building, Alaska Building, United States Government Building, Manufactures Building.

Reception areas in the Women's League Building (**TOP**) and the Hoo-Hoo House (**BOTTOM**) featured mission-style furniture and provided fairgoers with the chance to relax in a friendly, homey environment.

Theodore H. "Dad" Wagner's A-Y-P Band jumped into Lake Union on a dare wearing his heavy uniform and was rescued from drowning by crew members at the U.S. Lifesaving Exhibit, who were well practiced after weeks of daily public demonstrations.

King County strawberries, harvested in the Duwamish Valley and served with ice cream in cones baked by Seattle public school girls, were served by 20 Strawberry Queens elected by towns throughout the county. While enjoying their strawberries, fairgoers strolled through the King County Building and marveled at a new exhibit: a loaf of bread eight feet long, three feet wide, and two feet deep.

Because July 4 fell on Sunday, patriotic celebrations at the A-Y-P were held the following day. Suffrage leader Reverend Anna Howard Shaw held a Sunday meeting in the Auditorium Building, and the Seattle Symphony Orchestra performed in the Forestry Building. An evening concert featuring two hours of sacred music sung in Norwegian rounded things off.

Washington Day was also celebrated on July 5. The Washington State Building, bedecked with 14,000 Washington-grown roses, drew 20,000 fairgoers with a free lunch consisting of pickle, potted ham and chicken sandwiches, cake, ice cream, and lemonade. Nearby in the Good Roads Building the first-ever Congress of Good Roads went into session.

That evening Bud Mars attempted to pilot his Strobel airship directly over the crowded Pay Streak, flying so low that his path was actually hemmed in by the larger structures. His gas bag was impaled upon the flagpole on top of an attraction depicting the Civil War battle of the ironclads *Monitor* and *Merrimac*. The impact of the crash flung Mars 15 feet to the roof of the attraction, narrowly missing the 80-foot drop to the ground. Rushed to the Emergency Hospital where his injuries were pronounced minor, Mars told reporters that he'd wanted to give the crowd their money's worth. And crowd it was — 60,786, the largest attendance since opening day.

SERIOUS DISCUSSIONS

On July 6 a contingent of Filipino crewmembers from United States naval steamers *Dix* and *Burnside* visited the fair and formally protested the Igorrote Village attraction on the Pay Streak. Objecting emphatically to the implication that the nearly naked, dog-eating

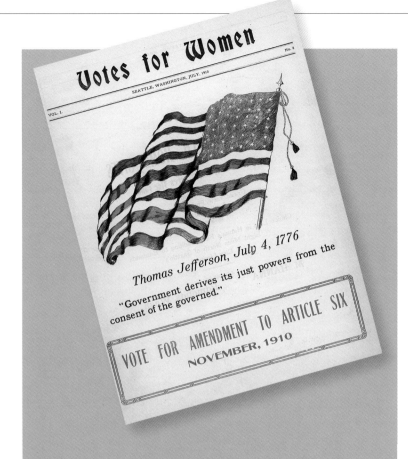

Votes for Women

SEATTLE, WASHINGTON, JULY, 1910

VOL. I   No. 8

Thomas Jefferson, July 4, 1776

"Government derives its just powers from the consent of the governed."

VOTE FOR AMENDMENT TO ARTICLE SIX
NOVEMBER, 1910

WOMAN SUFFRAGE

The year 1909 was a crucial one for proponents of Woman Suffrage in Washington. In January, state legislators placed on the November 1910 ballot an amendment granting women in Washington the right to vote and in the intervening time local, state, and national suffrage leaders threw their full weight into the effort to convince the state's male electorate to vote yes. In order to access the enormous crowds of potential voters who would be attending the A-Y-P, both the Washington Equal Suffrage Association and the National American Woman Suffrage Association held their conventions in Seattle in the first week of July 1909.

These conventions were widely covered in the local press. Suffrage leaders held a public meeting in the A-Y-P on Sunday, July 4, and celebrated A-Y-P Suffrage Day on July 7, 1909. The public exposure the suffrage cause received in conjunction with the A-Y-P was an important component in Washington women achieving the vote in 1910, and one step toward national woman suffrage conferred by the 19th Amendment to the United States Constitution in 1920.

Igorrotes were emblematic of all Filipinos, the crew members called the Igorrote exhibit "absolutely immoral and quite opposed to the elevation of human sentiment."

Wednesday, July 7 marked Woman Suffrage Day at the A-Y-P. Suffragists pinned green pro-suffrage emblems on nearly every incoming fairgoer — even on the exposition guards — and special balloons imprinted "Votes For Women" were sold and carried throughout the grounds. Banners with the slogan stretched over fair entrances. National and state suffrage leaders held a mass public meeting in the Auditorium Building, an afternoon reception in the Washington State Building, and a farewell dinner at The Firs in the YWCA Building. Suffrage Day provided crucial public exposure to Washington male voters and the female family members who would influence them, and was an important step toward Washington women achieving the vote the following year.

The Knights of Pythias, dedicated to promoting universal peace, also celebrated their Special Day on July 7. Meanwhile the performers in the Wild West show on the Pay Streak wanted frontier justice: Promoter Frank Watkins took off without paying them. *The Seattle Daily Times* claimed that the 10 Indians and two cowboys "have replaced their blanks with loaded shells." They wanted their money or they wanted revenge.

As Pacific and Chehalis counties celebrated their Special Days on July 8, controversy about the Igorrote exhibit continued to build, and exhibition officials continued to bungle their handling of the matter. President Chilberg decreed that, in the interest of decency, the Igorrotes would be given pants. Local newspapers pounced, chortling that this edict applied to tribeswomen as well as men — a shocking gaffe on Chilberg's part in that pants on Western women were unheard of, other than the barely tolerated bloomer garments some daring women wore when bicycling.

SPECIAL DAYS AND STATES

Thousands of Oregonians ventured north on their state's day, July 9, perhaps comparing the A-Y-P to Portland's 1905 Lewis and Clark Exposition, and saw for themselves the building their state had funded. The Portland Festival Chorus, 300-strong, gave a free performance in the Auditorium Building. An afternoon reception on the Oregon Building lawn was followed by a promenade and dance in the Washington Building. Buttons reading "Oregon, A-Y-P, 1909" were much in evidence.

The next day belonged to Kansans, who arrived at the fairgrounds in droves wearing sunflower badges and carrying covered baskets — a giant picnic was planned. Seattle Methodist Episcopal Church Bishop William A. Quayle had the crowd in stitches describing what he called the "Kansas microbe" — a germ that infected its host with a love of the Sunflower State.

Sigma Chi Fraternity men shared the Special Day. After a banquet in the New York Building, the brothers paraded to the Pay Streak, where their goal, wrote *The Seattle Daily Times,* was to "take in every show, ride every device in the streak, and abandon themselves to hilarious amusement." Alas, they did so in the heaviest rainstorm the fair had experienced since opening day. Perhaps by chance or perhaps due to the presence of so many Good Luck Billikens, weather at the A-Y-P Exposition had been mostly fair.

July 11 was a relatively quiet Sunday at the A-Y-P. The Five Juggling Jordans, a vaudeville act, gave two performances at the foot of the Pay Streak. Readers perusing *The Seattle Sunday Times* may have paused at a headline announcing "Igorrotes To Have Dog Feast" — but since the Igorrotes were portrayed as nearly naked dog eaters, recently savage, and barely reformed from head-hunting, many fairgoers expected this news. Although in their native villages these indigenous people consumed dog as part of a religious ceremony, local newspapers served it up salaciously.

Aeronaut J. C. Mars had his A-Y-P swan song on July 12. Exposition officials, dissatisfied with his recent performances, declined to renew his six-week contract.

At 10 a.m. the A-Y-P educational department began offering free educational tours to school-aged children — a boon to parents who wanted to see the fair at their own pace.

By the end of the day, A-Y-P attendance had passed the one million mark.

EARTHY MATTERS

More than 5,000 Whatcom County residents arrived in Seattle the next day to participate in Bellingham Day and Whatcom County Day. Proud Whatcomans gave away souvenir postcards bearing four-leafed clovers (the emblem of the county), cherries grown in Ferndale, and sample bags of fertile Whatcom County soil. The

BELOW: Igorrote men preparing dog as part of anthropological demonstration re-enacting a religious ceremony; **OPPOSITE PAGE, RIGHT:** Seattle pin-back button.

American Fisheries Company sent free passes to view their 12-acre salmon cannery in Bellingham.

San Juan County residents, not to be outdone, held their Special Day on July 14. Over 500 strong and accompanied by the Friday Harbor Military Band, they met President Chilberg at a reception in the Washington Building and boosted their county as they toured the exposition. The National Council of Women shared the day, holding the first public session of their convention in the Auditorium Building.

Exposition guards made the disconcerting discovery that nearly 100 men and boys had been sneaking into the fair each day through the North Trunk sewer line. Entering the eight-foot diameter sewer just outside the northeast corner of the fairgrounds, the culprits walked a quarter mile, clambered up an iron ladder, pushed up a manhole cover, and scrambled out into a clump of bushes near the Hoo-Hoo House. Guards had noted an increasing number of male fairgoers with dust on their backs — this discovery solved that mystery. Several young men were arrested but later released with strong warnings, and the manhole was secured under lock and key.

July 15 was designated United Amateur Press Association Day. The Washington State Press Association convention was in session, followed by the National Editorial Convention. Acknowledging the enormous debt of gratitude they owed the press for publicizing the A-Y-P, exposition officials showed the reporters a grand time and designated a series of press-related Special Days. Their efforts were apparently appreciated — *The Seattle Daily Times* reported that the press people "have neglected practically all convention business to see the fair."

That evening on the Pay Streak two bands of Indians from the A-Y-P Wild West Show — one from the Rosebud Sioux reservation and one from the Flathead reservation in Montana — watched dances at the Igorrote Village and then, according to *The Seattle Daily Times,* "turned loose a war dance." News of this display traveled quickly through the fairgrounds, drawing an enormous crowd. The Indians repeated

TOP: Philippine Building interior; **BOTTOM LEFT:** Forestry Building interior; **BOTTOM RIGHT:** Wooden program, National Lumber Manufacturers Association convention.

PRECEDING SPREAD: In the Manufactures Building visitors could sample coffee, tea, cereals, gelatin, strawberries and condensed milk, and popcorn, among other foods and could gather free souvenirs. Samples of malt tonic, a 5 percent alcohol concoction touted as medicinal, were particularly popular.

ABOVE: Children's Tours led by Seattle Public Schools teachers mixed learning with larking; **SURROUNDING:** Colorful postcards illustrate attractions on the Children's Tours.

EDUCATIONAL DEPARTMENT

The A-Y-P Educational Department was a free service available to school-aged children. Anna R. Miller and Elizabeth Carey, both Seattle public-school teachers, took groups of children through the fair, focusing on exhibits deemed educational. On the Pay Streak, the children saw the Battle of *Monitor* and *Merrimac*, the Battle of Gettysburg, and the Igorrote Village at greatly reduced prices. They saw the Eskimo Village, Baby Incubators, and Deep Sea Divers for free. In the Government Building they were given history and geography lessons as they viewed ship models, panoramas, and displays from the Smithsonian Institution. In the Hawaii Building they saw movies.

Parents could leave their children with the teachers and see the fair at adult speed. Children could enter the fair alone, take part in the school, and then roam the grounds unattended. The teachers put younger children on streetcars for the journey home, or, upon request, looked after them until someone was available to claim them. Anyone who had paid to enter the grounds could participate. Children who attended five sessions were issued a diploma.

YOU'LL LIKE TACOMA

THE LONGEST SHORELINE ELECTRIC SIGN IN THE WORLD
SEEN AT THE ALASKA-YUKON-PACIFIC EXPOSITION

ABOVE: Tacoma boosters installed an omnipresent electric sign along the Lake Union shoreline facing the exposition; **BELOW:** Tacoma pin-back button.

their performance at the Eskimo exhibit, after which they enjoyed a ride on the Ferris Wheel.

TACOMA, TEETH, AND TENTS

Banks, grocers, and many other Tacoma businesses closed on July 16, and some 15,000 Tacomans boarded steamships, train, buggies, and automobiles to Seattle and descended on the A-Y-P for Tacoma Day. More than 5,000 Tacoma boosters paraded through Seattle streets, the largest A-Y-P parade to date. *The Seattle Daily Times* noted with some surprise that women were among the marchers. Badges, sashes, and hatbands all sported the slogan, "You'll Like Tacoma."

Most of these citizens of Seattle's rival city had already seen the fair, but showed their community spirit by visiting again en masse. After a luncheon in the Washington Building the entire crowd moved from building to building, cheering as they went.

July 17 was Washington State Dental Society Day. The dentists and their family members paraded by automobile from their convention at Broadway High School to the A-Y-P grounds for a luncheon with President Chilberg and an afternoon of fair-going. Sailors and Marines stationed in Bremerton held a field sports meet in the stadium that afternoon. The late evening was devoted to recreating the Battle of Manila on Lake Union, with dazzling fireworks providing the rockets' red glare.

Meanwhile, The Mountaineers Club annual expedition to the summit of Mount Rainier departed Seattle. The party included Professor Edmond Meany, photographer Asahel Curtis, Washington suffrage leader Dr. Cora Smith Eaton, and many others. They carried with them an A-Y-P flag and a pennant reading "Votes For Women."

DOGS AND LOGS

On Sunday, July 18, as promised in the newspaper the week before, the Igorrote men roasted and ate a dog in their A-Y-P exhibit. Cambridge ethnology professor A. C. Hadden, guest lecturer in the University of Washington summer session, provided the animal, described by *The Seattle Sunday Times* as "a bashful, black, short-haired cur." Hadden's students looked on during the ritual.

San Bernardino (California) Day and National Education Day were celebrated on July 19. Sixty prominent loggers from Washington, Oregon, and California met in the Hoo-Hoo Building that morning to begin organizing the Pacific Coast Logging Association. The loggers felt that they were consistently slighted by the Lumber Manufacturing Association and needed an organization dedicated to facilitating and promoting the engineering and technical aspects of the logging industry.

Portland Day and Baby Christening Day were both held on July 20. The Portlanders, arriving on two chartered trains,

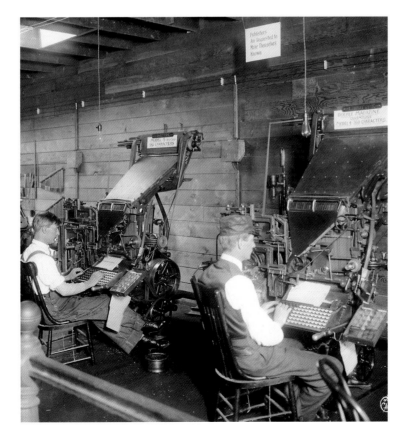

Linotype operators producing the *A-Y-P Daily News* also demonstrated the process to the public.

had several weeks earlier cancelled all of the ceremonies and activities scheduled for Portland Day, announcing that they just wanted to see the fair. The visitors wore buttons and ribbons and carried pennants bearing the slogan "Portland, 500,000, 1912." This signified the Rose City's population goal for that year (the city finally achieved it in the 2000 census). Oregon organizers had underestimated the number of Portlanders attending, and *The Seattle Daily Times* reported that "the supply of buttons, pennants, and ribbons was exhausted and many of the visitors were forced to wander around the grounds incognito. On account of the scarcity of these insignia, the souvenir hunters at the fair had an unusually hard day, and Portland badges were at a premium."

In the afternoon, 37 June-born infants were christened before a large audience in the Auditorium Building. A-Y-P Exposition President John Chilberg, Director General Ira Nadeau, director of ceremonies Josiah Collins, and director of special events Louis W. Buckley served as honorary godfathers.

On the Pay Streak that evening, members of the Seattle press corps entertained visiting press. "Foolishness will be a virtue and sorrow a crime," during the festivities, wrote *The Seattle Daily Times*. This foolishness included "clashes between exposition guards and the detectives, innocent bystanders being involved whenever possible . . . special spieling and raids on the concessions . . . summary execution of the ringleaders." President Chilberg and Director General Nadeau "threw all dignity to the winds" and donned Igorrote gee-strings (presumably over their conventional trousers).

FUN, THEN TROUBLE

On July 21 the state Medical Association celebrated its Special

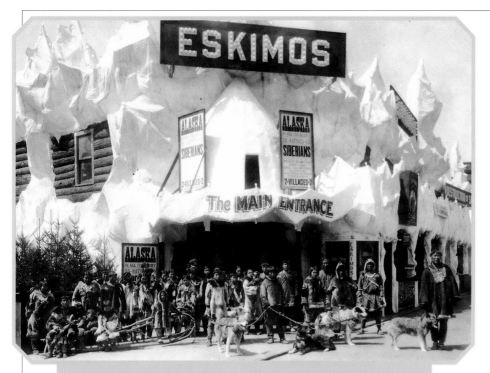

The Eskimo Village exterior was pure theatrics, but Siberian and Inuit performers demonstrated indigenous dress, crafts, and games with dignity.

AUTHENTICITY VS. THEATER

The Pay Streak tumbled re-enactments of real events (the *Monitor* and the *Merrimac*, the Battle of Gettysburg), representatives of seemingly exotic primitive people who were actively marketed as uncivilized (the Inuit/Eskimos, the Philippine Igorrote Tribe), premature babies who passively demonstrated the efficacy of as yet unconventional technology (the Baby Incubator Exhibit), entertainers with various degrees of subtlety, amusement rides, games of skill and chance, and all manner of carnival flimflam. As spielers along the strip strung out the ballyhoo, enticing fairgoers to part with their pennies, the line between authenticity and performance was muddled.

The Alaska Natives wore furs in Seattle's summer weather, posing in front of plaster icebergs; the Incubator Babies looked suspiciously robust; but the nearly naked Igorrotes cooked and ate real dog. Did fairgoers get what they paid for? The exhibits with historical or anthropologic connotations were major attractions, had been featured at many previous expositions, and were touted to visitors as highly educational. One of the lessons these attractions reinforced, almost certainly by design, was the superiority of the paying viewer over the participant/performers, and the pervasive belief that different meant other.

Day. Doctors attending the conference of the Medical Association of the Pacific Northwest and their families took a day away from their meetings to see the fair and enjoy dancing in the Washington State Building. The focus of the conference was fighting tuberculosis, a subject frequently in the news in Seattle as the recently formed Anti-Tuberculosis League of King County struggled to find a community willing to serve as the site for a facility for a much-needed tuberculosis sanatorium.

The Japan Building was dedicated and formally presented to the exposition before 2,000 invited guests that afternoon. Judge Thomas Burke, A-Y-P commissioners, members of the Mikado's imperial commission to the exposition, Japanese consul T. T. Kanaka, and many other dignitaries participated in the day-long ceremonies.

The Seattle Daily Times stated that special fireworks at the foot of the Pay Streak that night would include "electric water geysers, triple Gillouche wheels, dancing bears, performing clown, Hooligan, see-saw, silver falls, electric flashlight screen, welcome to editors, Japanese flag, A-Y-P-E shells, diamond-tail comet rockets, [and] aerial bouquet in A-Y-P colors."

The Order of Red Men and their auxiliary group, the Order of Pocahontas, celebrated their Special Day on July 22. The Red Men (all of whom were white) paraded through the fairgrounds in "Indian" costume, lunched in the New York Building with Great Chief Chilberg, and a put on what was billed as a sham battle in the stadium. The Red Men took the parts of Indians attacking a wagon train, whose members were played by members of the Washington National Guard. The women of the Order of Pocahontas retreated, no doubt with some relief, to an afternoon-long reception in the Woman's Building.

In a shocking turn of events, the sham battle turned fatal. Joseph H. Morhinway of Everett, leading a charge on the stage coach, was shot at close range with a wax bullet. The bullet penetrated his groin, severing his femoral artery, and he fell to the ground. Since many of the other actors were also on the ground feigning injuries, it was some time before the nature of Morhinway's trouble was discovered. Rushed from the stadium in the stage coach past the horrified crowd, Morhinway died of loss of blood at the A-Y-P Emergency Hospital.

JAPAN AT THE FAIR

Although the fair provided an opportunity to develop trade relations with Japanese businesses, racial prejudices in the larger society interfered with those efforts. Fair officials warmly welcomed Japanese businessmen and government representatives with ceremonies, a luncheon, and a banquet. Officers and a band from the Japanese naval squadron that came to Elliott Bay during the exposition participated in Children's Day activities. All public speeches emphasized hopes for a future of increasing connections between the United States and Japan.

These efforts reflected the alliance between the United States and Japan, and Japan's growing status as a world power.

In the months leading up to the exposition, however, anti-Japanese sentiment in the Washington State Legislature threatened the two countries' relations.

Legislators' ire focused on laborers coming into the country from Japan, but the legislation they considered discriminated against all Japanese. In January 1909, the legislators considered prohibiting all foreigners (though everyone knew the anti-Japanese intent of the bill) from carrying weapons. Then, in February, they considered introducing a law to require Japanese visitors to post bonds ensuring their return to Japan after the exposition. Such a bill would have created enormous difficulties for exposition, for city and state officials who hoped to welcome Japanese visitors to the fair, and for federal officials trying to maintain diplomatic relations with the government of Japan. At the behest of the State Department, Acting Governor Marion E. Hay intervened, asking the legislators to table the idea, which they did.

TOP CENTER: **A-Y-P officials and others pose under United States and Japan flags at the Japan Building dedication;** RIGHT: **Japanese women in kimono and their corseted western counterparts toast the Japan Building's dedication, July 21, 1909;** LEFT: **Japanese Village.**

ABOVE: Cake and coffee on the veranda conclude the American Women's League luncheon in the New York Building, July 15, 1909; BOTTOM: In the California Building the state trumpeted its walnut production with this giant elephant crafted from the nuts.

His accidental assailant was not known. Seattle coroner J. C. Snyder declined to hold an inquest.

OTHER DIVERSIONS

That afternoon's issue of *The Seattle Daily Times* reported that prominent Seattle citizens were trying to prevent Ringling Brothers' circus from setting up camp and potentially drawing audiences away from the A-Y-P. Cheyenne Bill's Wild West Show was currently attracting large crowds to performances in Seattle's Madison Park, while Luna Park in West Seattle remained a popular amusement destination (and served liquor), and vaudeville houses and small cinemas throughout the city gave fairgoers other places to spend their money.

On July 23, A-Y-P Exposition President Chilberg sidled briefly off the public stage to enjoy a week's vacation at Powell Lake in British Columbia, accompanied by his son Hugh. *The Seattle Daily Times* noted that Chilberg had arranged to take a wireless

telephone that had been displayed in the Manufactures Building along on his backcountry respite.

A luncheon for children who lived on the Pay Streak and appeared in various concessions enlivened the afternoon. The meal was held at the Nikko Café and hosted by Mary Miller, wife of John F. Miller, Seattle's Republican mayor. The children, who were of many different nationalities, wore the clothing of their native lands and carried flags as they were paraded through the A-Y-P grounds in rickshaws. Even one of the infants housed in the Baby Incubator exhibit attended — in the arms of his nurse, and eschewing the catered feast for his customary pabulum.

Readers of *The Seattle Daily Times* on July 25 enjoyed a full-page article entitled "What The Igorrote Thinks Of Us." The feature reported on an interview with Fa-Long-Long, one of the leaders in the Igorrote Village exhibition. Although infused with the Western reporter's ethnocentric cultural bias, the article touched on Igorrote marriage and family practices and described the economic gains of some of the Igorrotes on display at the A-Y-P. Fa-Long-Long stated that he received up to $5 per day in contributions from fairgoers, compared to the 2 cents per day he earned as a rice-grower in the Philippines.

Attendants pose with their charges in the Baby Incubator exhibit on the Pay Streak.

BABY INCUBATOR EXHIBIT AND CAFÉ

The Baby Incubator Exhibit drew Pay Streak crowds eager to view live human infants on display in an early type of incubator. Such exhibits had been featured at expositions since 1896. A-Y-P's added two unique twists: an attached Baby Incubator Café, and a babysitting service where, for a fee, fairgoers could leave their own infants while they visited the fair. Kny-Scheerer, a surgical supply company that manufactured incubators, held the contract, and the concession was managed by M. Edward Fischer.

The babies in the incubators may have been born somewhat prematurely, or may have been low-birth-weight infants born at term. The nine incubators held a steady temperature automatically and pulled in air for ventilation. Some of the babies were foundlings, and some may have been adopted during the course of the fair. Newspaper accounts make much of their widely ranging ethnicities. "Nurses" cared for the babies, and educational lectures were provided for visitors. Babies transitioned into a regular nursery, then graduated, and new babies replaced them throughout the course of the fair.

BEANS, BOTTLES, AND BEARDS

Fairgoers who toured the California Building on July 26 received one of the A-Y-P's more unusual commemorative items: gold stick pins set with real lima beans. These were distributed by representatives of Santa Barbara and Ventura. The Californians also passed out soft-shelled walnuts to celebrate their Special Day, which they shared with San Luis Obispo, Paso Robles, and Brooklyn, New York.

On July 27, the news of the day centered on the arrest of a recently discharged Vienna Café waiter by exposition guards. "Waiter Runs Amuck at A-Y-P Grounds," trumpeted *The Seattle Daily Times.* The waiter, Joseph H. Bock, was charged with assault and battery for allegedly attacking the Vienna Café's cook with a broken bottle, cracking it over his head and then hacking at his body with the jagged edges. This doubtless cost most dinner patrons their appetite. The *Times* was silent on the aftermath at the café — the

cook was taken to the Emergency Hospital and Bock was turned over to the Seattle Police.

Prompted by complaints from patriotic fairgoers, G. E. Mattox, who had replaced A. W. Lewis as director of concessions, ordered the management of the Japanese Village to immediately close the "Pull Uncle Sam's Whiskers" game. The amusement consisted of three plaster busts with hole-riddled chins through which strings protruded. Customers paid to pull a string and gain the prize tied to the other end. Mattox told the *Seattle Post-Intelligencer*: "Whether it is pulling whiskers from Uncle Sam's chin or feathers from the tail of the American eagle it cannot be practiced on the Pay Streak ... . It was a foolish game at best."

William Geddes, Commissioner for the United States Government to the A-Y-P, told *The Seattle Daily Times* that Seattle's balmy weather alone was enough to please fair visitors: "When I think of the torrid

LEFT: Fairground workers with permanent passes paid $2.00 to have their photograph attached, in order to come and go without charge; OPPOSITE PAGE: Wagner's A-Y-P Band poses on the steps of the Forestry Building.

COMFORT STATIONS AND RETIRING ROOMS

The official grounds plan for the A-Y-P indicates three public toilets (comfort stations): one in the far southeast near the Lake Washington boat landing; one just south of the Japan Building off Rainier Avenue; and one on the South Pay Streak next to Ezra Meeker's Pioneer Restaurant. On the second floor of the Washington Building were women's toilets and retiring rooms, and a men's toilet. The Government Building had public toilets, as did the Manufactures Building, Mines Building, and the Forestry Building, and it is likely that many of the other main buildings also offered this convenience.

The *Monitor* and *Merrimac* concession on the Pay Streak had public toilets. The YWCA restaurant included toilets and also retiring rooms for women, as did the American Women's League Building and the Washington Woman's Building. Retiring rooms gave women a home-like place to withdraw from the frantic hustle of the fair. Typically outfitted with comfortable chairs, couches, and cots, some retiring rooms also had cribs where a baby could safely rest while its mother caught her breath or soothed a cranky toddler. These private female-only spaces also gave mothers a clean, private spot to nurse their infants.

ABOVE: Nattily dressed Elks pose in front of A-Y-P Official Photographer Frank Nowell's studio;
RIGHT: A parade moves past the Chinese Village and Ferris Wheel on the north Pay Streak.

heat of the St. Louis and Chicago expositions, I know how the visitors from the broiling East must appreciate a visit to this cool retreat, where the weather is always bright, but never hot."

PIGGY'S PARADE

July 28 was a Special Day for the Brotherhood of Elks, and for Port Townsend. More than 600 Port Townsend residents playing hooky from work arrived en masse on a chartered steamer, the *Iroquois,* and paraded to the Washington Building accompanied by the Sixth United States Artillery Band. This well-respected group was attached to Fort Warden.

About 2,500 Elks, rollickingly high-spirited and dressed in carnival clothes to publicize the circus they were holding that afternoon, paraded to the grounds from downtown Seattle accompanied by a dozen brass bands. Piggy, a little dog who made a name for himself as the adopted mascot for the A-Y-P, trotted alongside the marching Elks. Marchers at various points in the formation hoisted banners reading "Piggy Is Coming," "Piggy Is Here," and (as the wagging black tail receded into the distance) "Piggy Has Went."

Ferris Wheel manager Len Pearson, an Elk himself, invited the brotherhood to use the wheel as headquarters for the day. *The Seattle Daily Times* reported, "A lot of those who had brought their youngsters with them turned the wheel into a day nursery and had Manager Pearson lock them safely in the cars while they went out to report to the marshals of their various divisions. As long as the wheel kept moving the youngsters were happy."

The implacably sincere members of the Woman's Christian Temperance Union paraded through the A-Y-P grounds at 1 p.m. Accompanying them were 500 children, all members of the W.C.T.U.'s Loyal Temperance Union junior auxiliary, who performed drills and songs. Members of the W.C.T.U. wore white ribbons, the symbol of their cause. The prohibition against alcohol sales on University of Washington property and thus at the A-Y-P made the day especially satisfying for the temperance advocates, who told *The Seattle Daily Times* that the A-Y-P's "law and order and high morality," attributed by them to lack of alcohol, would doubtless result in future dry expositions.

The Elks, meanwhile, mounted two circus performances in the Exposition Stadium before a combined crowd of 20,000. Capacity for the venue was 8,000 — it must have been standing room only. The circus performers, all Elks and many prominent members of their communities, were costumed in drag, some in black face, some as clowns, and some as menagerie animals. The happy, hungry crowd devoured the available concessions — hot dogs went like hot cakes. At 8 p.m. the electricity failed, plunging the exposition grounds, Elks and all, into dusk. The Temperance crowd had adjourned a reception at the Woman's Building at 7, and must have thanked providence yet again for the A-Y-P's absence of alcohol.

SWEDES INDEED

Members of The Mountaineers expedition reached the summit of Mount Rainier the morning of July 30. In the midst of a howling wind, they planted a staff bearing an A-Y-P flag and a Votes For Women pennant. Both blew down immediately. They were carried up Columbia Crest and planted in the snow, but after a few minutes they blew down again and the staff was broken by the wind. Eventually the flag and pennant were placed inside the crater and left there when the party descended.

COPYRIGHT-1909,
BY
ASAHEL CURTIS

86

President Chilberg, born in Iowa to Swedish immigrant parents, returned from British Columbia to be on hand for July 31, when the A-Y-P celebrated Swedish Day. Despite the fact that a delegation of Swedish Day organizers and exposition VIPs had traveled to St. Paul earlier in the month to beg him to participate in Swedish Day, Minnesota Governor John A. Johnson was a no-show. Part of the confusion was that the date for Minnesota Day had originally been set for August 14, but was then changed to August 3. Johnson cancelled a planned Chautauqua lecture tour so that he could be in Seattle for Minnesota Day, but later said had never planned to arrive in time for Swedish Day.

Swedish Day organizers, however, were planning on his presence. On the very morning of the event the *Seattle Post-Intelligencer* stated that Johnson's train would arrive at noon and he would be escorted to the grounds in a 30-car procession. His scheduled 2 p.m. address in the Natural Amphitheatre was to be the "dominant feature" of Swedish Day. His train arrived — a day later. Fair Vice President Richard Ballinger, Washington Governor Hay, and Chilberg filled in as speakers in front of the crowd of 17,000 who had gathered to hear Johnson. Johnson's failure to reach Seattle in time for Swedish Day was perceived as an affront to the local Swedish community, and Chilberg was a leading critic.

Swedish Day racked up 40,352 admissions — considerably higher than the average daily attendance during the rest of July. Festivities began with a parade in Swedish national costumes. At 2 participants enjoyed a special Swedish Day program in the Natural Amphitheatre. That evening the United Swedish Singers, some 250 voices strong, joined with a soloist from Stockholm to dazzle the crowd. Washington's sizeable Swedish community had spent months organizing details for Swedish Day, and its success was considered a resounding triumph.

By the time the last Swedish Day visitors had gathered their pennants, postcards, and sleepy children, and made their way to the streetcar station, 1,531,664 people had visited the fair — 861,275 of them in July, an average of 27,783 each day. Written about in newspapers and magazines around the country, flocked to by Washingtonians and visitors from near and far, the A-Y-P was the place to be.

INSET: Jubel Kantat program; **LEFT:** A view taken from Capitol Hill across Lake Union shows the exposition in all its glory.

AUGUST 1909

THE A-Y-P GOES NATIONAL, WITH A 12-MINUTE FILM ON THE EXPOSITION DISTRIBUTED TO THEATERS IN MAJOR CITIES AROUND THE COUNTRY. AN INTREPID GROUP ARRIVES BY CAR FROM LOS ANGELES — AN 18-DAY TRIP. A 60-FOOT REPLICA OF A VIKING SHIP SAILS IN FOR NORWAY DAY AND KAISER WILHELM SENDS HIS GREETINGS FOR GERMAN DAY. ONE OF THE HIGHLIGHTS OF THE MONTH IS THE HEATED CONTEST FOR THE TITLE OF CARNIVAL QUEEN.

EXCEPT FOR THE MUSIC OF THE SEATTLE SYMPHONY Orchestra, United Swedish Singers, and Canadian Bugle Band, August 1 was a relatively quiet Sunday at the A-Y-P. Special Days were still being assigned even as the fair entered its third month, and Seattle newspapers trumpeted a growing list of governors, senators, captains of industry, and other VIPs who were still expected to attend.

To the joy and relief of exposition management, the United States Senate appropriated $30,000 to pay for 25,000 more electric light sockets and bulbs in the Government, Hawaii, Philippines, and Alaska buildings, which had among them only 6,000 lightbulbs. Because most funding for these government buildings had been spent on construction, the exposition had installed limited lighting at its own expense, hoping that a federal appropriation would be forthcoming.

Many Americans unable to attend the A-Y-P would soon experience it via film shot during opening day on June 1. Among the theaters where the 12-minute film was to be screened were the Majestic in Chicago, the Ramona Park in Grand Rapids, the Orpheum in New Orleans, the Forest Park Highlands in St. Louis, and the Orpheum in Salt Lake City. It was anticipated that 25,000 moviegoers would see the film each week.

ABOVE RIGHT: Norway Day medal; OPPOSITE PAGE: Souvenirs were one way fairgoers could take their A-Y-P experiences home.

PROFESSIONAL PHOTOGRAPHERS

Frank H. Nowell served as the official photographer of the A-Y-P. He provided images of the fair to accompany the thousands of publicity articles sent to the national media by the exposition company and produced postcards that visitors eagerly purchased as souvenirs and as a way to share the experience with folks at home. Other professional photographers sold photographs of the fair, although none as extensively as Nowell. Nowell had made his name in photography in Nome, Alaska, where he opened a studio after years of work with his father in a mining company. After the fair he remained in Seattle, opening a studio downtown.

Photographer Frank Nowell's self-portrait reflected in a gazing ball.

BOTTOM LEFT: Alkali Ike's Wild West and Indian Show performers gather for a ballyhoo; **BOTTOM RIGHT:** Gee-string investigators (from left): Judge Thomas Burke, Igorrote Village manager R. C. Schneidewind, Washington Governor Marion Hay, Reverend Mark Matthews, A-Y-P President John Chilberg, and Igorrote Village manager John Kreider with child performer Wy-il; **OPPOSITE PAGE:** King Street Station.

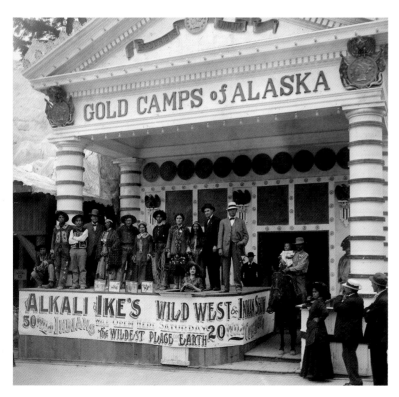

On the Pay Streak, Ferris Wheel concessionaire Len Pearson put his machine through its paces for a skeptical party of mechanical engineers. Pearson demonstrated the wheel's ability to be safely and quickly unloaded during electrical outages via a series of brakes.

Farther down the Pay Streak the Igorrotes were also safe — from persistent do-gooders who badgered authorities to force them into Western clothing. The *Seattle Post-Intelligencer* reported that Washington Governor Marion Hay, President Chilberg, Reverend Mark Matthews, the outspoken pastor of Seattle's First Presbyterian Church, and Thomas Burke, a respected jurist, inspected the concession, met with Igorrote Village managers, and officially agreed that the villagers could continue to wear the exposition-provided gee-strings rather than pants.

GOVERNORS GALORE

New York Governor Charles E. Hughes visited the fair on August 2 to lead New York Day celebrations. Hughes went directly from his train to the fairgrounds on Sunday evening and spent the night in the New York Building. By the time he emerged on Monday morning a crowd of several hundred had gathered on the lawn. Hughes greeted these well-wishers, and then set off with his wife, Antoinette, and New York State Senator Benjamin Wilcox.

Although Hughes planned to tour the grounds, Alaska A-Y-P Commissioner J. C. McBride waylaid him in the Alaska Building, sat him down with coffee and a serving of canned Alaska salmon, and delivered a lecture on the intricate workings of the newly invented salmon-processing machine. News of Governor Hughes's presence drew a crowd whose curious members pressed toward the glass door and gawked at Hughes and his wife as they listened and nibbled.

The luncheon that followed his tour boasted the presence of three additional governors: Washington's Marion Hay, West Virginia's William E. Glasscock, and Minnesota's John Johnson. Chilberg had accused Governor Johnson of a calculated slap to local Swedes for having failed to arrive in time for Swedish Day. This omission, Chilberg insisted, would hurt him politically. *The Seattle Daily Times* reported Johnson's response: "It is a matter of absolute indifference to me what President Chilberg thinks."

JAMES J. HILL

After James J. Hill bought the St. Paul & Pacific Railroad in 1878, with plans to take the line west to the Pacific coast, his critics predicted his ruin. Competing transcontinental lines already existed and Hill's route traveled through sparsely populated country. Undeterred, Hill built his line in small increments — with no government aid — and attracted small farms and homesteads along his path before moving on. The process took years, but after his line — the Great Northern — reached Seattle in 1893, he was well on his way to being a very wealthy man.

Within a few years he bought the competing Northern Pacific line, and soon began adding other railroads to his empire. Hill's successes helped the Northwest timber industry, and Hill was also one of the earliest industrialists to recognize the importance of Pacific trade.

In 1906, Hill opened King Street Station in Seattle, which became the main portal for those visiting the A-Y-P three years later. Because the Empire Builder played such an important role in the economic development of the Northwest, Hill was asked to deliver the keynote speech on opening day. An enormous bust of Hill was dedicated on the fairgrounds. It is now located next to More Hall on campus.

FROM EVERETT TO OLYMPIA

On August 3, thousands of men, women, and children from Snohomish County paraded through downtown Seattle, then marked Snohomish County Day at the exposition. A large banner carried in the parade read "Seattle is a suburb of Mukilteo." Everett residents had planned to join the march carrying 50 smokestack replicas in tribute to their city's industrial capacity. A devastating fire changed their plans. It had swept through Everett the previous afternoon, quickly followed by a string of arson fires. Twelve buildings, including the Snohomish County Courthouse, stood in ruins, and weary Everett residents who'd spent the night guarding their homes from firebugs skipped the A-Y-P festivities.

At 3 p.m. the bronze bust of Empire Builder James J. Hill, a gift to the University of Washington from the people of Minnesota, was unveiled on Klondike Circle. Many in the large crowd that gathered to watch knew Hill personally. The railroad magnate was credited with making A-Y-P possible by virtue of his importance to Washington's economic development. That day Governor Johnson spoke in the Auditorium Building, and that evening experienced the A-Y-P honor of having his portrait displayed in fireworks over Lake Union.

University of Washington regents spent almost the entire day touring the grounds, developing a list of buildings they would like to keep after the fair ended.

Many communities gave away commemorative ribbons as part of their Special Day observations, but on August 4 Olympia chose to hand out 10,000 cactus dahlias, the A-Y-P Exposition's official flower. Shelton also celebrated a Special Day on August 4. Unwilling or unable to compete with Olympia's

cascade of blossoms, Shelton residents told exposition officials that they would simply see the fair together, adding, "We are small, but we can paddle our own canoe."

ALASKA CHILDREN AND WOMEN

A committee busy planning for the August 20th Pay Streak Day invited the public to mail in ballots and elect a Carnival Queen who would reign over the day's festivities. *The Seattle Daily Times* printed a ballot and instructions to mail it to the committee's headquarters at Ye College Inn, 40th Avenue and 14th Street. Real-estate promoter Charles Cowen built the inn just a block from the exposition's main gates to house A-Y-P visitors.

L. A. Thompson, inventor of the popular Scenic Railroad concession installed on the Pay Streak and at many other locations throughout the world, was in Seattle to visit the fair and see his masterpiece in operation. Calling Thompson a millionaire, *The Seattle Daily Times* enthused, "In all its history of twenty-five years throughout the experimental period down to date there has not been a broken bone or drop of blood spilled from the millions of patrons of this splendid but thrilling amusement devise."

Thursday was Alaska Children's Day, and children from Alaska were admitted free. The youngsters started their day at 10 a.m. with refreshments in the Alaska Building, then moved on to the Hawaii Building for yet more edibles. The staffs of the California, Utah, and Education buildings all wanted to provide lunch for the children, but Mary Hart, the Alaska Women's Auxiliary member who organized the day, demurred, citing the many snacks. An all-expenses-paid visit to the Pay Streak gave the children a chance to burn off steam. Back in the Alaska Building, Skagway resident Gladys Kirmse entertained the children by playing the first piano carried over Chilkoot Pass to the Klondike — like the miners, it traveled to the gold fields.

RIGHT: The six-foot bronze bust of James J. Hill sculpted by Finn Frolich was a gift to the University of Washington from the people of Minnesota; OPPOSITE PAGE: In mid-July the women who worked as hostesses in the exhibit buildings and the wives of fair commissioners organized the A-Y-P Hostess Association.

Chehalis County (the future Grays Harbor County) published a colorful booklet to distribute at the fair.

While on the Pay Streak the children no doubt noticed the day's tallest VIP: Eight-foot, four-inch George Auger, sometimes called the "Cardiff Giant," slipped away from his headline engagement in *Jack, The Giant Killer* at the Orpheum Theatre to see the fair. He posed for photographs in the Igorrote Village.

The next day was devoted to Alaska women and was an important opportunity for women's auxiliaries to show the public a different aspect of Alaska womanhood from that of gold-rush profiteer or Gold Camps of Alaska dancing girls who frequently lined up to ballyhoo on the Pay Streak. *The Seattle Daily Times* reported, "Anyone who has an idea that Alaskan women are shiftless individuals with disheveled hair, careless and poorly clad, would have learned different today ... . Mrs. Mary E. Hart, organizer of the auxiliaries, says that their purpose primarily is to prove to residents of the states that the Alaska women are cultured."

Women who attended the Alaska Women's Day/National Hostess Association luncheon in the Alaska Building arrived to find the balcony area converted into an ersatz mining camp. They watched demonstrations of sluicing and panning for gold, and enjoyed a camp-style lunch of pork and beans. Louis Buckley led them to the Woman's Building, where Director General Ira Nadeau formally welcomed them. They then proceeded to the Pay Streak.

SLOGANS AND STEAMBOATS

On August 6, more than 2,000 residents of Chehalis County (later renamed Grays Harbor County), sporting badges reading, "You'll Take To The Tall Timber," arrived for their Special Day. Hoquiamites added their own badge, which read "Hear Hoquiam Hum." Elma sent a delegation bravely bearing banners that promised, "You Can't Beat Elma." Everyone expressed approval of their own Chehalis County Building and the many lumber exhibits it contained.

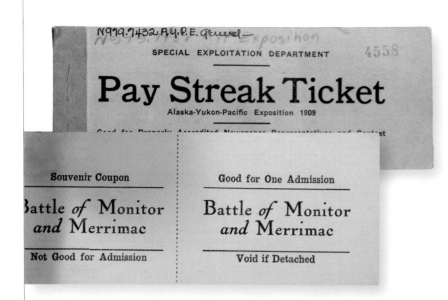

SPECIAL EXPLOITATION DEPARTMENT

4558

Pay Streak Ticket

Alaska-Yukon-Pacific Exposition 1909

Souvenir Coupon	Good for One Admission
Battle *of* Monitor *and* Merrimac	Battle *of* Monitor *and* Merrimac
Not Good for Admission	Void if Detached

Won't You Stroll With Me On the Pay-Streak?

WORDS BY KARL KNAPPEN

MUSIC BY SOL. LEVI.

PUBLISHED BY THE EMPIRE MUSIC PUB. CO.
316 KOHLER—CHASE BLDG. SEATTLE.

TOP: Newspaper reporters were issued free tickets to Pay Streak attractions;
BOTTOM: Fairgoers could recapture A-Y-P memories by purchasing exposition-themed sheet music to play at home.

Not to be out-badged, 3,000 Illinois Day celebrants sported buttons that read, "I'm A Sucker," a nod to the nickname often given to residents of that state.

A performer in the Igorrote Village, given permission by concession management to cut handles for the spears the "villagers" sold on the Pay Streak, combed the shore of Lake Washington and then, growing hungry for lunch, knocked on the door of a nearby house. The woman who answered the door, reported the *Seattle Post-Intelligencer,* "left the savage grinning at the front door while she went out the back on a hot foot for the nearest telephone. From then on both the exposition guards and the city police were deluged with cries for help from frightened householders." Apparently pursued throughout the afternoon, the man was eventually escorted back to the fairgrounds.

Meanwhile Mr. and Mrs. George Harrison and friends arrived at the A-Y-P from Los Angeles in their 1908 Locomobile, having accomplished the remarkable feat of navigating the entire route without being forced to ship the car by rail due to bad roads. It took them 18 days to do it. One stretch of their route included 30 miles of bone-jarring corduroy (logs laid crossways). On their best day the party traveled 165 miles.

In Renton on August 7 even the coal mines stood idle so residents could enjoy Renton Day at A-Y-P. Two steamboats, the *Fortuna* and the *Urania,* each carried 350 passengers in a thrilling race up Lake Washington from the Renton dock to the A-Y-P dock. *Urania* won by 100 yards, making the 15-mile trip in a record-setting 47 minutes. Street cars and Interurban trains were crowded with more fairgoers making their way north, and upon arrival they toured the grounds boosting Renton. Meanwhile 1,000 Seattle Business College alumni swarmed the stadium, where they held races, field day events, and a baseball game.

FROM HIGH TO LOW

Stakes in the Carnival Queen contest got higher with real-estate developer Ole Hanson's announcement that the winner would receive a $300 residence lot on the east side of Lake Washington. Eskimo Village performer Columbia Eneutseak, known as "Miss Columbia," led the pack with 926 votes, with Maud Thomas of Seattle in a distant second at 102 votes.

LEFT: James Lacy's Dixieland Spectacle Band and show troupe on the Pay Streak. The performance featured traditional plantation songs and dances and was the most visible example of African-American participation in the fair;
BOTTOM LEFT: One of the performers at the Spanish Theatre and Jardin De Paris was Nellie Brown, the "Dancing Cockney"; BOTTOM RIGHT: Female performers in the Alaska Theatre of Sensations don robes over their scanty costumes but show a little leg all the same.

That evening a Northern Pacific Special carried the proud Mountaineers party home from their successful journey to the summit of Mt. Rainier.

Lyman J. Gage, who had been president of the World's Columbian Exposition, spent Sunday August 8 touring the A-Y-P ground with his granddaughter Cornelia Pierce. He gave the fair high marks.

A woman accused of shoplifting a bracelet from a booth in the Oriental Building was sent to King County Jail that afternoon. It was the exposition's first reported shoplifting attempt.

Down in Portland, minister J. Whitcomb Brougher preached on the evils of some Pay Streak concessions, as he had perceived them on a recent visit to the A-Y-P. "There are some things on the Pay Streak at the A-Y-P Exposition that are worth seeing," he was quoted in *The Seattle Daily Times*. "But the vulgarity which characterizes many of the exhibitions shows the low moral standard of those who visit them, and is a sad reflection upon our beautiful suburb, Seattle."

SPREADING GLEE

On August 9, 161 Angelenos, most of them Chamber of Commerce members, were welcomed to the A-Y-P for Los Angeles Day at a morning reception in the California Building. The boosters, wearing

The Temple of Palmistry on the Pay Streak.

THE WICKED FAIR

Concerned that girls and women who ventured to the A-Y-P Exposition would be vulnerable to molestation of various sorts, the Young Women's Christian Association (YWCA), Woman's Christian Temperance Union (WCTU), and International Welfare Protective and Rescue Association (IWPRA) all made efforts to secure the physical and moral safety of females at the fair. IWPRA set up a tent city where females who worked at the fair could live. WCTU hired Mary Brown, famous for her public lectures on purity, to maintain a presence on the fairgrounds and protect unchaperoned young women.

The YWCA provided traveler's aid to women arriving alone to Seattle by train, and the City of Tacoma hired three female police officers to assist women at train and boat docks in that city. Doubtless some, but probably not all, of this help was appreciated. Protecting women from perceived procurers who might seduce them into prostitution or kidnap them into white (or other) slavery also meant curtailing their freedom of movement and perhaps editing the way female visitors experienced Washington, Seattle, and the fair.

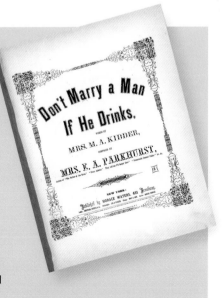

**"Don't Marry A Man If He Drinks"
was a catchy temperance ditty.**

Oregon Trail preservationist Ezra Meeker reads a newspaper amongst the waitresses at his Pioneer Restaurant on the Pay Streak.

EZRA MEEKER

Oregon Trail immigrant Ezra Meeker was a Washington pioneer who made — and lost — a fortune raising hops in the Puyallup valley. Meeker was a prolific publicist for Washington Territory and then for the state, promoting the region's bounty to Eastern newspaper publishers and with the nascent Northern Pacific Railroad as early as 1870. In 1885 he was Washington Territory's representative to the American Exposition in New Orleans, Louisiana, and in 1886 served the same function in London at the Colonial and Indian Exposition.

In 1891, Meeker was elected executive commissioner of the Washington World's Fair Association committee, which was planning Washington's participation in the 1893 World's Columbian Exposition, but clashed so mightily with fellow commissioner Edmond Meany that he was relieved of his post. After four unsuccessful attempts to find gold in Alaska, Meeker turned his attention to retracing and marking the Oregon Trail — which by 1906 was vanishing — and lobbying for its preservation. This mission would consume him until his death in 1928.

By 1909, Meeker's fame was such that A-Y-P Exposition Director General Ira Nadeau gave him a substantial footprint on the Pay Streak at no charge. Meeker, his oxen, Dave and Dandy, and his prairie schooner (covered wagon) were popular sights on the exposition grounds.

"Go To Beautiful Seattle And Enjoy Life" buttons, toured Puget Sound and visited Tacoma during their week-long jaunt.

By that afternoon Miss Columbia had garnered 2,057 votes in the Carnival Queen contest. La Belle Baya followed with 500 votes, and Pauline Evans with 158. No matter who was crowned, exposition guard P. A. Chapman would not be around to protect her: Chapman's sergeant discovered him fast asleep only three hours into his shift. His stick and badge had been stolen while he slept. Taken directly to Chief Wappenstein, Chapman was immediately dismissed.

The National Association of Park Superintendents, meeting in Seattle and celebrating a Special Day at A-Y-P on August 10, were so impressed with the fair that they suggested the grounds be preserved as a public park. Apparently unfazed by the fact that the land belonged to the University of Washington, some local residents began pursuing this plan.

A crowd of former New Englanders gathered at King Street Station on Wednesday August 11 to welcome a 100-member party from Worcester, Massachusetts. The group included the famous Worcester Glee Club, which sang "Auld Lang Syne" punctuated with "Seattle!" and "Worcester!" as they detrained. The trip from Massachusetts had evidently been just as gleeful. Worcester Board of Trade Secretary John L. Sewall told *The Seattle Daily Times* that every minute of the week-long trip had been a single round of pleasure. The Worcester Glee Club performed twice daily at A-Y-P through the remainder of the week.

The New England Society hosted a dinner for the visitors from Worcester at the Puritan Inn on the A-Y-P grounds the next night. Downtown Seattle cafés reported that the influx of New Englanders was stimulating a run on corned beef and cabbage.

The Glee Club performances were surely featured on the new circus-bandwagon-style advertising streetcar that the Seattle Electric Company put into service in early August. The brightly painted car boasted panels on each side advertising upcoming A-Y-P attractions. It played music as it traveled along streetcar tracks through downtown Seattle and out into the residential districts.

The A-Y-P was even advertised in the sky after the arrival of the largest captive balloon in America. The balloon was tethered behind Ezra Meeker's concessions on the Pay Streak. (Besides this captive balloon, at various times this entrepreneurial pioneer of the Oregon

Trail ran a restaurant, a Joy Wheel, and a Wild West show.) Riders on the captive balloon, outfitted with telescopes and field glasses, rose dramatically to 1,500 feet above the fairgrounds.

VETS AND VIKINGS

Friday, August 13, was Manila Day. Festivities were centered on the Philippine Building. The day marked the 11th anniversary of the fall of Manila during the Spanish-American War, and several in the crowd had participated in the battle. These veterans may have been the best judges of the fireworks display put on by the Los Angeles Fireworks Company at the foot of the Pay Streak that evening: It depicted the bombardment of Moro Castle at Santiago de Cuba, and must have been clearly visible from the Igorrote Village.

Unlike his sleeping former co-worker, Exposition Guard J. McDonald was overzealous in his duties that evening. According to *The Seattle Daily Times,* McDonald "laid violent hands" on a man he apprehended committing the grave offense of stepping onto the manicured grass. Unfortunately for McDonald, the culprit was Exposition Director General Ira Nadeau, who was rushing toward a reported fire in the Auditorium Building. McDonald's punishment was one night's suspension.

Miss Columbia, meanwhile, was up to 8,054 in the Carnival Queen contest. Maud Thomas held second with half as many votes. Alma Zahl trailed a long list of hopefuls with one (hopeless) vote.

August 15 marked the maiden voyage of the historically accurate reproduction of a 60-foot Viking ship that would carry the Sea King, his Queen, and their attendants from Bothell, where the ship was built, to the fairgrounds for Norway Day later that month. The ship, manned by 40 "Vikings," was launched in the afternoon. Artisans

were still busy painting Viking shields in the Beaux Arts studio in the old University of Washington building in downtown Seattle.

TICKLED PINK

On the Pay Streak, the management of the Fairy Gorge Tickler was pleased to announce that its concession cars (really more like barrels) had just been fitted with rubber bumpers. This promised a much smoother ride: "No more are combs to jump out of women's coiffures. No more are hats to fly from men's heads as they double up with laughter on the 'Tickler,'" claimed *The Seattle Daily Times.* Other

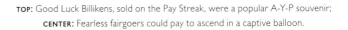

TOP: Good Luck Billikens, sold on the Pay Streak, were a popular A-Y-P souvenir; **CENTER:** Fearless fairgoers could pay to ascend in a captive balloon.

ABOVE: Runners start the mile relay in the military athletic tournament in the A-Y-P stadium; BELOW: Brass button from A-Y-P police force uniform;
OPPOSITE PAGE: Performers in the French Fete on August 23 rehearsed for weeks.

Pay Streak concessions also had honed their public pitches. The Ferris Wheel's display advertisement in the *Times* boasted, "Safer in the air than on the streets — GO! around — around — and around." The Spanish Theatre, meanwhile, advertised something just as dizzying: "Nothing but clever Girls — Girls — Girls. Nellie Brown, The Singing Cockney, Sisters Masqueria, Dainty Matilda, Dorine, and a score of other Live Wires."

Fay Masqueria, one of the Masqueria Sisters, joined the race for Carnival Queen and zoomed up the tally list to third place, garnering 4,502 votes on Sunday, August 16, alone.

Channing Ellery's Band, a popular group that had appeared previously at the Jamestown and Lewis and Clark expositions, began twice-daily performances at the Music Pavilion that afternoon. These concerts would continue to attract crowds until the fair closed in October.

Baron Kogoro Takahira, Japan's Ambassador to the United States, visited the fair that same day and was feted with a luncheon in the New York Building. *The Seattle Daily Times* printed Takahira's remarks about how past expositions had benefited trade between Japan and the United States. It also printed his prediction, indicative no doubt of Japan's current imperial preoccupations, that, "If there is ever to be a war between us it will be entirely of a commercial nature, and it must be fought out fairly and gentlemanly."

MISS COLUMBIA

Columbia Eneutseak, better known as "Miss Columbia" or Nancy Columbia, was born on January 16, 1893, on the World's Columbian Exposition grounds in Chicago, and named by wealthy socialite Bertha Honore Palmer. Columbia's teenage mother was part of an Inuit group from Labrador performing in that fair's "Eskimo Village," work she continued to perform with Columbia and other family members over subsequent decades.

Attired in seal-skin pants, beaded mukluk boots, and a caribou parka, Miss Columbia was an exposition veteran by the time she appeared at A-Y-P, and Pay Streak royalty even before she was voted Carnival Queen in a highly publicized August 1909 contest. She hosted formal receptions at which she granted interviews to the press, conversed with her fans, and signed autographs. Although anthropological exhibitions at A-Y-P, as at other expositions, reinforced broad stereotypes, Miss Columbia pushed this boundary and established a more individual public identity. Miss Columbia's vibrant photogenic persona was probably one reason that the Eskimo Village became one of the most popular — and lucrative — Pay Streak concessions.

Queen of the Pay Streak Columbia Eneutseak (right) and her mother, Esther Eneutseak.

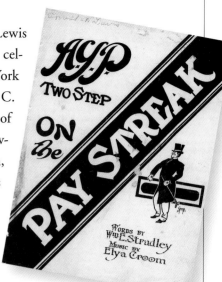

On August 17, more than 2,000 Lewis County residents arrived by train to celebrate Centralia Day. In the New York Building Nebraska Governor A. C. Shallenberger addressed hundreds of former Nebraskans who were observing their Special Day. That afternoon, Madame Yale, who advertised herself as "the world renowned celebrity whose rare beauty baffles description," gave a free Physical Culture Matinee and Beauty Culture Lecture in the Auditorium Building.

Crowds lined 2nd Avenue in downtown Seattle on the morning of August 17 to watch the largest A-Y-P parade thus far make its celebratory way toward the fairgrounds to mark German Day. Kaiser Wilhelm reached out from the Fatherland with a cablegram sending German-Americans celebrating German Day his highest greetings. During the athletic contests that afternoon the audience was encouraged to sing along with a German patriotic anthem, "Die Wacht Am Rhein." An afternoon Ladies Reception was prelude to an evening of German music enjoyed by what was described as the largest crowd ever packed into the Auditorium Building. Celebrants then danced the night away. *The Seattle Daily Times* summed things up: "Teutons Have Best Day Of All."

A-Y-P attendance passed the two-million mark around noon on Wednesday, August 18.

QUEEN OF THE PAY STREAK

Two Streets of Cairo performers, La Belle Baya and Cheriff Sechri Effendi, were married (or, perhaps, "married," since such public weddings were often for show and not legally binding) on the Pay Streak at 9 that evening. Advertisements for the event promised "Gorgeous Oriental Ceremony — Many handsome souvenirs will be distributed." The usual 25-cent admission, of course, was charged.

Meanwhile the race toward the Carnival Queen crown heated to boiling point when Seattleite Maud Thomas, long a distant second behind Miss Columbia, somehow garnered 10,516 votes during the course of the day. With only hours left in the contest, this brought her total to within several hundred of Miss Columbia's. On Thursday, the wait was over: Miss Columbia, age 16, emerged victorious with 58,410 votes. Maud Thomas came in second with 50,968 votes.

August 20 was Pay Streak Day, and featured the biggest list of free attractions thus far. The day began with the arrival by barge of Her Majesty Miss Columbia and her court at the landing at the foot of the Pay Streak. Wearing a robe and crown, Miss Columbia led a parade composed of Pay Streak performers of more than 20 nationalities through the grounds to the stadium. Athletic events had a carnival flair: chariot, freak, cowboy, and animal races, and a tug-of-war between the Eskimo and Igorrote villagers. A scheduled race between two hot-air balloons went awry: one balloon rose only 20 feet and as it careened across the field one of its dragging cables hit Miss Columbia, who fortunately was unharmed.

Old Fiddlers tried to out-fiddle one another on Klondike Circle. A young woman performed what was billed as a Dive for Life — sliding down a long cable into Lake Washington on a pulley she clenched between her teeth. A couple from the Japanese Village was married on the Ferris Wheel, and San Jose, Californians, Lottie Holmes and J. T. Lanfall wed one another in the captive balloon. A water carnival on Lake Union combined with a lifesaving demonstration were afternoon features. The evening included a Beauty Parade of All

ABOVE: Of all the wonders that beckoned fairground visitors, none captivated imaginations more than the Pay Streak; OPPOSITE PAGE, RIGHT: The Pay Streak inspired many musical tributes, including this two-step.

Nations, a dance contest between the many varieties of Pay Streak dancing girls, and a special fireworks display.

STAGEHANDS, SCOTS, AND SCOFFLAWS

The Theatrical Mechanics Association and Interstate Improvement Club were also honored on the 20th. In order that their various shows might go on, members of the Theatrical Mechanics Association started their Special Day at 11 p.m. — after the final curtains in local vaudeville houses had been rung down. Festivities began in front of the Spanish Theatre, where John Chilberg and Ira Nadeau were initiated as honorary members of the association.

Caledonian Day on August 21 began dramatically as a flaming cross was carried through downtown Seattle accompanied by bag-pipers and drummers summoning everyone of Scottish descent to don their kilts and join the parade to the A-Y-P. Vancouver, British Columbia, dedicated a temporary arch at 3rd Avenue and Marion Street and turned it over to the city of Seattle. Upon arrival at the grounds, the crowd watched 1,000 children weave ribbons around a spectacular maypole. Bagpipe and dancing competitions, sword dances, and many athletic events followed. An evening concert in the Natural Amphitheatre featuring marches and reels by the Vancouver Pipe and Drum Band and Scottish songs by the Ralston Male Glee Club was enjoyed by all. That same day the French Fete, a *tableaux vivant* of nineteenth-century French life, was presented in the Auditorium Building.

The A-Y-P guards, meanwhile, arrested and jailed Seattle police officer G. A. Bergstrom who, with a team of other officers, had been invited to participate in the tug-of-war competition and

BELOW: Performers in Alkali Ike's Wild West Show pose in the arena behind the Gold Camps of Alaska concession.

Amateur photographer C. E. Meldrum's snapshot captures Miss Columbia (center) and other Eskimo Village performers as a ballyhoo spieler exhorts the Pay Streak audience to step right up.

HAND-HELD CAMERAS

For the burgeoning legion of amateur photographers, the A-Y-P was paradise. At many other major fairs the public had been prohibited from using cameras or had been charged a fee to bring in smaller cameras. Some world's fairs went so far as to evict camera-holders or to issue orders requiring guards to smash any camera smuggled in. This proved particularly difficult for fairgoers who had traveled some distance with their camera, unaware of the prohibitions, and were then faced with the maddening and inconvenient question of what to do with the camera if they wanted to enter the fairgrounds.

A-Y-P fairgoers, in contrast, were welcome to bring onto the grounds, free, any camera not larger than 6 1/2 by 8 1/2 inches. This included the very popular Brownie camera, introduced by Kodak in 1909 and the first mass-marketed camera. Exposition officials, many of whom had extensive experience at other fairs and thus with the public-relations headaches the camera issue could create, calculated that welcoming smaller cameras would gain the A-Y-P credit with fairgoers. Camera supplies were sold on the grounds and fairgoers could also have their film developed. Frank H. Nowell was granted the official A-Y-P photographic concession to produce and sell large photographs on the A-Y-P grounds.

promised free passes to the fair. When the police team arrived at the main gate there were no passes waiting, and when Bergstrom tried to walk over to the Administration Building to sort things out the guards arrested him for not paying. It took an hour for an exposition official to spring the irate Bergstrom from the clink, and when he was finally free he and his team declined to tug and left the grounds.

Later that afternoon six bucking broncos from the Wild West show broke out of their corral and dashed up and down the crowded Pay Streak. Several fairgoers were knocked down but no one was seriously injured.

The Seattle Daily Times announced on the 22nd that since they had been put on sale the day before, 30,000 souvenir tickets to September 6 Seattle Day had been sold. The paper also mentioned that President Chilberg and Concessions Director Mattox were being held in contempt of court for their failure to appear in King County Court the day before. Chilberg and Mattox were being sued by the management of the Dizzle-Dazzle concession because of their unwillingness to permit the Dizzle-Dazzle to replace the unpopular Giant Piano concession on the Pay Streak.

TEARING DOWN, SPRUCING UP

On Monday morning workers began tearing down the stadium north grandstand to make way for the next month's stock show.

Shoppers in downtown Seattle enjoyed intricate Norwegian folk costumes created for the upcoming Norway Day on display in the windows of the Bon Marché Department Store.

Myrtle Seattle, granddaughter of Chief Seattle and a student at the United States Indian School in Tulalip, cooked and served lunch for Julia Ballinger, wife of Richard Ballinger (whom Taft had recently appointed secretary of interior) and her friends. The meal, described by *The Seattle Daily Times* as, "an appetizing, up-to-date luncheon [far removed from] … the crude course dished up to the warrior who gave the city its name," was intended to demonstrate how successfully (according to the prevailing attitude of the time) the Indian School experience had erased traditional ways. The luncheon was a feature of the Congress of Educators of Indians that was taking place during the last week of August.

The International Beauty Day contest also held that day promised the most beautiful woman on the A-Y-P fairgrounds a $150 diamond-studded gold watch. At 9 that morning, members of a secret committee began working their ways individually through the buildings, grounds, and Pay Streak scouting out the fairest at the fair. The judges' approach to potential beauties was sometimes rebuffed by the young women or their chaperones — one judge trying to speak to a girl being pulled in a rickshaw with her mother was taken for a masher. Twenty women between the ages of 16 and 20 were eventually given cards inviting them to appear as finalists at 4:30 in the Auditorium Building. Sixteen showed up, and Edith Klopf, a 17-year-old Seattleite, was declared the winner in front of an audience of more than 1,000.

MAKING HAY

Current and former residents of 14 Southern states gathered to celebrate Dixie Day on August 24. Then, at an afternoon reception in the amphitheatre, Washington Governor Marion Hay opened his mouth. He told the crowd how pleasantly surprised he had been on a recent Southern visit to discover so many intelligent people living there. "I had always thought the South to be more or less indolent, thriftless, and profligate," *The Seattle Daily Times* quoted him as saying. Dixie Day organizers, the paper said, "blushed for Hay" while visiting Southerners could not believe their ears. They managed somehow to move past the remark, and that evening a large crowd enjoyed dancing amid decorative cotton bales and southern flowers in the Washington State Building.

On August 25 the first of many, many A-Y-P Exposition prizes was awarded by jury. The American Woolen Company took top honors for its worsted wear. A deluge of judging continued through the rest of the exposition.

Free pineapple was served to those who attended a morning reception in the Hawaii Building that day, and anyone who visited the building also received a free bag of raw sugar. The Troubadours

of Hawaii passed through the grounds handing out favors and flowers. Princess Kawanakoa, whose husband, David, was a member of the Hawaiian royal family, was an honored guest at the festivities.

Meanwhile, 2,000 Utah residents arrived by train to help dedicate the Utah Building, and fez-clad heads bobbed throughout the fairgrounds as the Mystic Shriners celebrated their Special Day.

More than 250 uniformed Salt Lake City High School cadets drilled in formation on August 26, impressing fairgoers. The boys were in the midst of an eight-day encampment on the University of Washington grounds, and were participating in the day's joint Salt Lake City/Ogden/Provo/Logan Special Day. In the auditorium the first National Conservation Congress got underway.

Special Events Director Louis Buckley resigned his position in order to take up the same job at the Portola Carnival, opening in San Francisco on October 19. Buckley planned to help out with Seattle Day, New England Day, and Exhibitors' Day before departing in mid-September.

DENNYS AND DAHLIAS

More than 200 people aged 80 and older were honored on Octogenarian Day on August 27. Three prominent celebrants were Seattle founders: 82-year-old Louisa Boren Denny, her 86-year-old sister Mary Ann Boren Denny, and their 84-year old brother Carson Boren. Mary Ann Boren Denny was awarded a gold clock for being the oldest early resident of Washington in attendance.

ABOVE: A-Y-P Jurors evaluated produce, handcrafts, artwork, manufactured goods, and livestock, awarding medals and diplomas; OPPOSITE PAGE, TOP: Hawaiian officials, hostesses, and musicians pose in front of the Hawaii Building, August 24, 1909; OPPOSITE PAGE, BOTTOM: Conservation Congress pin-back button.

CONSERVATION CONGRESS

The first National Conservation Congress, organized by the Washington (state) Conservation Association in response to the Report of the National Conservation Commission issued in January 1909, met at the exposition from August 26th to 28th. The nearly 100 attendees included delegates from state conservation commissions, university representatives, church leaders, and delegates from commercial organizations. Session topics included irrigation, soils, good roads, mining, forestry, "and the relation of Capital to Labor in the work of general conservation of natural resources."

Gifford Pinchot, a prominent conservationist who strongly advocated the principle of "wise use" as the first chief of the Forest Service from 1905–1910, spoke at the congress. The congress ended with a religious service on Sunday, August 29.

That afternoon the first of four Welsh Eisteddfod choral competitions was held in the Auditorium Building.

"Made-In-Washington" promotions were a special feature of Manufacturers' Day on August 28, culminating in a dinner where only products of the state were served. The menu included a number of sweets: ice cream flavored with Crescent Manufacturing's Mapleine, a popular maple flavoring; candies from both Superior and Imperial candy companies; Albers Brothers' Violet Oat cookies; and raspberries in Pacific syrup. For those who preferred smokes over sweets, the Mike Wright Company provided cigars.

Cactus dahlias, the official flower of the A-Y-P Exposition, were honored on the same day. The blooming plants so thoroughly decorated the Washington State Building that it seems surprising fairgoers could wedge themselves in, too. More than 35 growers submitted their dahlias for judging, and every fairgoer received a blooming cactus dahlia.

NOTES AND NORSEMEN

The Mormon Tabernacle Choir, at A-Y-P for Utah festivities and to compete in the Eisteddfod, refused to perform when they realized that, like the other competitors and like the audience, they would be charged 75 cents each to enter the venue. Exposition officials were livid — the 125-member choir had been admitted to the fairgrounds free of charge. By default they awarded the $1,000 main choral prize to Seattle's St. Mark's Episcopal Choir. The following evening the Mormon

Tabernacle Choir sang, for a financial compensation, before a non-paying audience in the Natural Amphitheatre.

And, busily boosting Seattle and the upcoming Seattle Day, the city's Chamber of Commerce and the Seattle Day Committee distributed, with the help of local businesses, 50,000 Seattle Day buttons, asking each "loyal citizen" to wear one.

August 30 was Norway Day, and it proved to be one of the A-Y-P's most memorable Special Days. At 12:30 crowds gathered at the foot of the Pay Streak to watch the Viking ship, which, according to the advance press in *The Seattle Daily Times,* would sweep "majestically around the bay off Laurelhurst. . . . The Vikings will discover the exposition grounds and make their landing on the new Vinland at 12:30." Astrid Udness of Bellingham, Norway Day's Queen, Jennie Johnson of Tacoma (Queen Margredhe), and Inga Latson of Seattle (The Peasant Bride) met them and led a procession to the stadium. There they formed a pageant/parade representing nine periods in Norse history. The afternoon was taken up with a major musical presentation led by the St. Olaf College Band. The United Norwegian Singers of the Pacific Coast performed along with a number of well-known soloists that evening in the Natural Amphitheatre for a crowd of 20,000.

Michigan Day was celebrated on August 31. Governor Fred Warner of the Wolverine State was unable to attend, but he sent two large cheeses. Samples were given out at the Michigan Club Building to the delight of the cheese-lovers in the crowd.

The month ended on a sad note when Edna Clark, aged 18, collapsed and died in the arms of her younger brother, Colberg, on the morning of August 31. The siblings, who lived in Bellingham, had been enjoying the fair together when, in the Oriental Building, Edna fell into Colberg's arms. Colberg's cries attracted help, and as strangers carried his sister into a booth he ran from the building in

ABOVE: Utah medallion; **CENTER:** Norway Day commemorative ribbon; **OPPOSITE PAGE:** Crowds gather to watch a parade on the esplanade at the foot of the Pay Streak.

search of their father. Dr. Mark Ward McKinney ran over from the Emergency Hospital, but found Edna lifeless. Her death was attributed to heart disease, the same ailment that had killed her mother several months before.

Passing through exposition gates during August were 901,711 people, generating receipts of $263,872.75. The month's most popular days were German Day (38,642 visitors), Norway Day (42,026 visitors), and Pay Streak Day (43,139 visitors). Across the nation, people were talking about Washington and the A-Y-P.

ABOVE: The *Official Daily Program* sold for a dime each day; **RIGHT:** Dome Circle near the northeastern fairground boundary. From left: Idaho Building, Spokane County Building, Chehalis County Building, with Denny Hall visible in upper right.

SEPTEMBER & OCTOBER 1909

Seattle Day is hugely successful, drawing the largest crowd of any single day of the fair. But don't count out the Smiths. Thousands of them turn out for Smith Day, wearing buttons saying, "I am a Smith; Are You?" A huge livestock show proves a hit and President Taft arrives to tour the exposition, attracting a crowd of nearly 61,000. Crowds continue to pour through the turnstiles in October as the fair winds down to a bittersweet conclusion.

September at the Alaska-Yukon-Pacific Exposition started with a bang. As the sun set on September 1 Wisconsin Day festivities, crowds gathered at the stadium to watch a new fireworks spectacle presented in part by Seattle-based Hitt's Fireworks. The show, entitled "The Destruction of Mexico," was held every night until September 15.

On the field, 10,000 square feet of scenery depicted Mexico City under Aztec rule. At each performance more than 150 men portraying Hector Cortez's Spanish conquistadors laid siege to the city. By the end of the hour-long

OPPOSITE PAGE: Fairgoers stroll the paths in the Court of Honor.

fireworks extravaganza, the city was in ruins. Unlike the actual city, it was rebuilt in a day for the next night's show.

GREEN AND GREY

On Thursday, September 2, famed botanist Luther Burbank visited the A-Y-P to give a speech, something he usually refused to do, claiming that his field was agriculture, not public speaking. He also refused to talk to the press unless they paid him $10 an hour. The *Seattle Daily Times* shelled out, whereupon Burbank mostly bragged about his accomplishments and chastised his critics.

Also that day, a delegation of 36 Japanese businessmen visited the A-Y-P during a two-week tour of cities around Puget Sound.

After a luncheon at the Formosa Tea House, they toured the Pay Streak, where the entire party took in the *Monitor* and *Merrimac* exhibit. Every member claimed to be very well-read in American history, and they vigorously applauded at the end of the recreated naval battle.

But the people who had the most fun that day were those named Smith. Anyone with that last name was given a purple badge bearing the words, "I am a Smith; Are You?" All of the Smiths (along with Smythes, Schmitzes, Schmidts, and other variations on the name) marched in a special Smith Day parade, heard a lecture about famous Smiths, and participated in contests to see who was the youngest, oldest, tallest, fattest, thinnest, prettiest, and homeliest Smith in attendance. Director General Nadeau declared this Special Day "the most spirited celebration we have had yet."

Earl Grey, Governor General of Canada, visited the fair with his family on Friday, having just returned from a trip to the Yukon. Also on the grounds were more than 2,700 visitors from Wenatchee, to celebrate their Special Day. Most of them arrived by train aboard the Big Red Apple Special wearing badges that read, "You'll Do Better in Wenatchee."

Japan Day was celebrated on September 4 starting with a parade in downtown Seattle, followed by a lawn party at the fairgrounds in

Smith Day contest winners.

Actual Gettysburg veterans vouched for the concession's veracity.

MILITARY MIGHT

Two of the more popular concessions along the Pay Streak gave visitors a chance to relive the Civil War through the recreation of two of its more famous fights — the maritime battle between the *Monitor* and *Merrimac*, and the Battle of Gettysburg. Both exhibits placed the viewers in the center of a gigantic cyclorama — a cylindrical panoramic painting — as if they were standing in the center of each historic event.

The *Monitor* and *Merrimac* exhibit was the more complex of the two, with mechanical and electrical effects that were considered very high-tech for their day. The electrical control room inside the building contained more than 125 switches and rheostats that controlled the movement of the ships as well as lighting effects from sunrise to sunset. A highlight of the show was a terrific storm, complete with rain, wind, and lightning.

The Battle of Gettysburg depicted Pickett's Charge, the climactic Confederate attack on the Union army. A sign outside the building read, "War! War! War! Replete With the Rush, Roar and Rumble of Battle." Inside, the painting measured 27 feet high and more than 350 feet in circumference, and during each show a lecturer pointed out key scenes in the battle. A similar cyclorama of this exhibit still exists, and has been restored at Gettysburg National Military Park in Pennsylvania.

front of the Japan Building. After lunch, crowds filled the auditorium to hear speeches by local Japanese-American business owners and community leaders. A formal reception was held in the Washington Building that evening.

SEE YOU ON SEATTLE DAY

Sunday was relatively quiet, but only because most people were anticipating the next day's events. For months, exposition officials had been planning for the one day that would draw the largest crowds — Seattle Day. Tens of thousands of advance commemorative tickets bearing Chief Seattle's image were sold, special badges were manufactured, and store owners were urged to close up shop so that the entire city could come and join in on the festivities. The goal was to have 200,000 people walk through the gates.

At 8 in the morning on September 6, a volley of shells was fired over Lake Union, signaling the start of Seattle Day. An 8-year-old boy was first through gates. Even President Chilberg stowed his pass and waved a souvenir ticket as he made his way through the turnstiles. All morning long, streetcar after streetcar dropped off visitors. Most folks brought their own lunches, expecting long lines at the A-Y-P cafés and restaurants.

A military parade made its way through the fairgrounds, leading the way toward the Natural Amphitheatre, where city officials made short speeches. After a rousing version of "The Star Spangled Banner," the crowd dispersed.

Some went to the stadium to take in the athletic events. Others walked down to the shores of Lake Union to watch canoe races between representatives of Indian tribes from British Columbia and around Puget Sound. Most people checked out the Pay Streak, and some enjoyed the warm weather by sitting in the shade, watching the people go by.

In the early evening, thousands returned to the amphitheatre to hear a competitive concert between choruses representing Great Britain, Sweden, Norway, Ireland, Denmark, Scotland, Wales, and the United States. The highlight of the show was a performance by a children's chorale made up of more than 1,000 boys and girls.

ABOVE: Pin-back button boosting Seattle Day; **BELOW:** Re-enactors disembark the *"Mayflower"* on New England Day, September 11, 1909.

Sadly, the children's finale had more than a touch of pathos. George Bech wrote the official Seattle Day Song, "Old Glorious Glory," and for weeks had helped the children practice singing it. As fate would have it, Bech died the night before its debut. His young protégées hung their heads in sorrow as they sang, and the crowd bared their heads in tribute.

Meanwhile a special boat carrying King Rex and Queen Anne Quality arrived at the foot of the Pay Streak, kicking off a Mardi Gras parade. Merry and carefree revelers rang cow bells, tooted horns, and tickled passersby with feather dusters. The carnival continued until the fair closed for the evening.

After sundown, Channing Ellery's Band performed the "Damnation of Faust" at the Geyser Basin. The surrounding buildings turned off their lights, and spotlights played upon the scene in the basin. The Devil and dozens of imps scurried and scampered, and pyrotechnics created a dramatic effect.

The day ended with fireworks. Besides the Destruction of Mexico spectacle at the stadium, thousands of skyrockets were fired over Lake Union, and a variety of ground displays lit up the waters below.

Seattle Day was a huge success, drawing the largest crowd of any A-Y-P day. About 118,000 people were on hand to celebrate. Still, this fell far short of the 200,000 that everyone hoped for. Had Seattle Day been held on a day other than Labor Day, the number might have been greater. Instead of going to the fair, union workers held their own celebration at Woodland Park, where more than 12,000 people enjoyed a picnic and a day at the zoo.

Nevertheless, exposition officials were pleased with the Seattle Day turnout. And even with all those throngs of people at the A-Y-P, the day's only mishap was when some unlucky fellow slipped on a custard pie and twisted his ankle.

GENERAL MAYHEM AND GENERAL SEWARD

On Wednesday, September 9, thousands attended California Day festivities and enjoyed free fruit given out at the California Building. Things got out of hand when workers began tossing fruit into the crowds. Some people got bonked by stray peaches and oranges, a few of which burst, splattering juice everywhere. Notwithstanding that messy affair, no one left until the last peach had been given away.

TOP: Seattle Day souvenir ticket; **BOTTOM:** The South Entrance Gate featured a pastiche of quasi-Asian, quasi-Northwest Native styles and was adorned with numerous electric lightbulbs; **OPPOSITE PAGE, INSET:** The United States Postal System issued a commemorative A-Y-P 2-cent stamp bearing William Seward's likeness on A-Y-P Opening Day; **OPPOSITE PAGE, RIGHT:** William Henry Seward statue.

The Hoo-Hoo men picked September 9 (9/9/09) as Hoo-Hoo Day in honor of their mystical number nine. Worn out from a late night initiation ceremony and boxing match the night before, the Hoo-Hoos began their celebration at 1 p.m. with a baseball game, followed by a general meeting at the Hoo-Hoo House, an evening dance, and then a raucous trip to the Pay Streak.

On September 10, the statue of William Seward was dedicated in front of the New York Building, a fitting location since the structure was a replica of Seward's mansion in Auburn, New York. General W. H. Seward, the statesman's son, gave a stirring speech in which he recounted his father's efforts in securing the United States purchase of Alaska from Russia. The statue was unveiled by little Harriet May Baxter, granddaughter to former Washington Governor John McGraw, who was also in attendance.

PLAYMATES AND PILGRIMS

On Saturday, September 11, the fairgrounds were filled with youngsters celebrating King County Children's Day. Anyone under the age of 15 was admitted free, and exposition management left it to the boys and girls to be truthful about their ages. Some came with their parents, but many attended alone. About 100 local women volunteered that day to look out for the safety of the large number of unaccompanied children.

A free vaudeville circus was held at the amphitheatre, and afterwards clowns and jugglers wandered the fairgrounds adding to the fun. Most kids headed to the Pay Streak. To their surprise and delight they discovered that an anonymous group of 12 Seattle businessmen had purchased thousands of various ride and amusement tickets, and had instructed Reverend W. A. Major and Lincoln High School Principal James E. McKown to hand them out to any boy or girl who appeared unlikely to have enough money to enjoy the day.

It was also New England Day, and in the afternoon a cannon salute of 13 shells drew crowds to the shores of Lake Union to welcome a reproduction of the *Mayflower* coming in under full sail. On board were 102 members of the local New England Club, all dressed

WILLIAM HENRY SEWARD

On April 9, 1867, the U.S. Senate ratified the purchase of Alaska from Russia, in a vote that barely passed the two-thirds majority required for approval. Russia was reluctant to sell and the United States was reluctant to buy. The dealmaker for this hard-fought treaty was U.S. Secretary of State William H. Seward. At the time, most Americans thought that $7.2 million was too steep a price for land that was considered almost worthless. The territory became known as "Seward's Folly."

A year before he died, Seward was asked what act of his would be most remembered by the American people. "The purchase of Alaska," he stated, "But it will take another generation to find it out." That they did in 1897, when gold was discovered in the Klondike region, greatly elevating the economic stature of Alaska, and the Pacific Northwest.

By the time of the A-Y-P, Seward was a hero. Before the fair, the postal service issued a 2-cent A-Y-P postage stamp which bore Seward's likeness. And at the fair, Seward's son helped unveil a statue of his famous father. After the exposition, Judge Thomas Burke wanted the statue moved to a prominent location in Seattle's Pioneer Place, but eventually it made its way to Volunteer Park, where it has stood ever since.

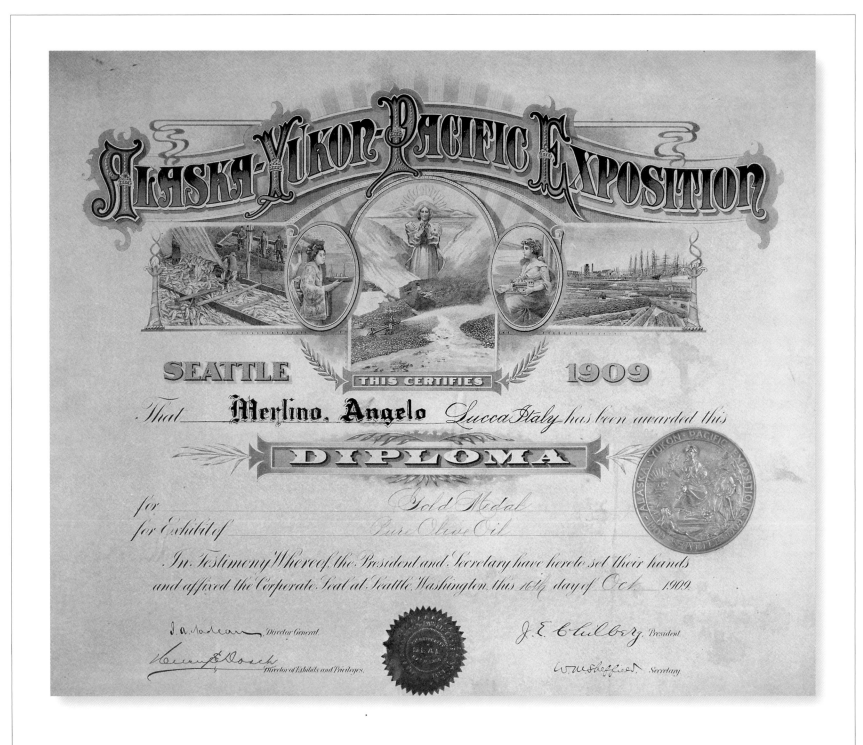

ALASKA-YUKON-PACIFIC EXPOSITION

SEATTLE 1909

THIS CERTIFIES

That **Merlino, Angelo** *Lucca Italy has been awarded this*

DIPLOMA

for *Gold Medal*

for Exhibit of *Pure Olive Oil*

In Testimony Whereof, the President and Secretary have hereto set their hands and affixed the Corporate Seal at Seattle, Washington, this 16th day of Oct. 1909.

Director General.

Director of Exhibits and Privileges.

J. E. Chilberg, President.

W. M. Sheffield, Secretary

Among the thousands of manufactured products competing for prizes at the A-Y-P was Angelo Merlino's olive oil, which was awarded a gold medal.

China Day participants wear a dragon costume during a parade.

of parade marchers, and a Chinese orchestra atop a float playing drums, cymbals, and stringed instruments.

President Chilberg escorted Imperial Chinese Consul Goon Dip to the stage during a formal gathering at the auditorium. Chilberg addressed the crowd, noting how proud he was to see the Chinese community share in the "Seattle Spirit." Goon Dip passed along greetings from the "oldest nation to the youngest and strongest" and noted how much the Chinese appreciated the friendship of the American people.

Black educator and activist Booker T. Washington was supposed to visit the fair around this time, but his work at the Tuskegee Institute in Alabama kept him from attending. Exposition officials had tentatively scheduled an "Afro-American" Day timed for his arrival, but it never came to pass, even though Washington's wife, Margaret, and son Booker T. Washington Jr. visited. Margaret Washington attended a luncheon hosted by members of Seattle's African-American community, and discussed her belief that black women, in general, were being neglected.

HAVING A BLAST

Farmers and ranchers throughout the Northwest were present in abundance this week. Ellensburg, Vashon Island, and Boise, Idaho, celebrated their Special Day on September 14. The next day, trainloads of Southeastern Washingtonians arrived to take part in Adams County Day, and on September 16, Governor James Brady arrived from the Gem State to take part in Idaho Day festivities. Brady spoke of the wide-open spaces ripe for development in his state, inviting the "landless man" to move out to the "manless land."

Earlier that morning, a baby was born in the Igorrote Village to Sey-e-nec and Pat-ta-wik, who had reportedly fallen in love a year earlier. At a private ceremony a few days later the proud parents named their newborn boy "President Taft." Needless to say, the press was quickly informed of this moniker.

On the night of September 17, about 6,000 people gathered at the foot of the Pay Streak to witness a re-enactment of the *Gaspee* affair, a precursor to the Boston Tea Party. The *Mayflower* from New England Day had been remodeled to represent the *Gaspee*, and at the beginning of the program, 12 men dressed as Indians snuck out to the ship and began tossing crates over the side.

in Puritan garb. After a re-enactment of the landing at Plymouth Rock, the pilgrims held a reception in the auditorium. A reception and dance at the Washington State Building that evening capped the day.

At some point over the weekend, Piggy the exposition dog went missing. It wasn't until later in the week that Chief Wappenstein got a call from the Seattle police. Poor Piggy had lost his collar, engraved with the words, "A.Y.P.E. Mascot, Piggy," and was picked up downtown as a common vagrant. Luckily one of the arresting officers recognized the famous pup.

CHINA DAY AND A VISITOR FROM ALABAMA

China Day was celebrated on Monday the 13th with two parades, one downtown followed by another at the exposition. Seattle's Chinese-American community arranged both parades, which included participants from San Francisco, Portland, Victoria, and Vancouver. The pageant featured an elaborate painted dragon carried by dozens

After the boarding party returned to shore, a battery of cannons fired live ammunition at the doomed vessel. The sloop of war caught fire, and flames soon climbed up the rigging. The masts fell just as the fire reached the magazine. With a roar that could be heard around the city, two cases of powder exploded inside the hull, sending chunks of the vessel high into the air. The crowd cheered and the A-Y-P band played on.

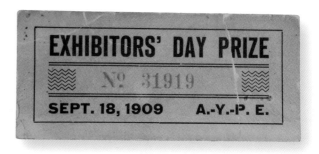

SOMETHING FOR NOTHING

Saturday, September 18, was Exhibitors Day, one of the most popular days at the fair. More than 61,000 people attended and almost all walked home with a free gift. Each person who passed through the gates received a coupon with a number. Each exhibitor building had a placard with numbers on it, and once the visitor found the right one, they had to go inside and visit the booths until they found their prize.

Items ranged in value from 50 cents up to hundreds of dollars. Prizes included $25 tea sets from the Japanese Building, a mahogany rocking chair worth $50 in the King County Building, baskets of fruit, boxes of honey in the comb, and even an all-expenses-paid train ride through Alberta and British Columbia.

It was noted that winners had to accept what they won, or else turn it down. If an 8-year-old girl won a pair of work boots, or some burly longshoreman won a dainty sunbonnet, so be it. The only break from this rule came from the California Building. If a temperance advocate won a free bottle of wine, it could be traded for something more befitting.

The biggest prize on Exhibitor's Day came from Stevens County — a homestead with running spring water and a good supply of timber. Possibly the strangest giveaway was a month-old baby boy named Ernest, described by *The Seattle Daily Times* as "the property

TOP LEFT: Prince Albert the Educated Horse was a last-minute substitution for a more famous equine act, Princess Trixie, who died just before the fair opened; **TOP RIGHT:** Each Exhibitor's Day ticket could be traded for a prize; **BOTTOM:** Ag-o-nai, a performer in the Igorrote Village, and her infant, named Washington, who was born during or just prior to the A-Y-P.

Crystal, fruit, nuts, and (even though the A-Y-P was "dry") wine were on display in the California Building.

of the Washington Children's Home Society." The holder of that winning ticket had to have the proper qualifications demanded by the society, and had to express interest in adopting the child. There is no record of anyone claiming little baby Ernest.

Most people were happy with their prizes, but Tacoma resident Chillman White was an exception. White was so upset with whatever he won that he printed up 3,000 badges with a ribbon reading, "To Hell With Seattle, I'm Going Home," and a few weeks later tried selling them on the fairgrounds. Chief Wappenstein confiscated the lot, and told him to stop being such a grouch.

PENNSYLVANIANS AND CANADIANS

On Sunday, news came from Pennsylvania that a new transcontinental automobile relay run was delayed due to an accident. The auto race in June had attracted so much attention that the *Philadelphia*

Press sponsored a new run, bearing a message from President Taft. Less than a day after it began, the first relay car flipped over near Reading, Pennsylvania, killing the courier. A new car was sent out a week later.

On September 20, the fairgrounds were full. Italians from all over the state, including a contingent of coal miners from Carbonado and Black Diamond came to celebrate Italy Day. Multitudes of mail workers gave their stamp of approval to Postmasters Day activities, and former residents of Canada's Prince Edward Island celebrated their Special Day.

Canadians were also on hand the next day to celebrate Edmonton Day. But pride turned to dismay when residents of the Alberta city discovered that signboards, placards, and even *The Seattle Daily Times* announced that it was "Edmonton, B.C." Day. T. W. Brown, director of the Alberta exhibit, was described by the *Seattle Post-*

LEFT: Statue of Northwest pioneer Marcus Whitman; RIGHT: Horses were among the thousands of animals judged during the livestock show.

Intelligencer as being an "indignation meeting within himself," giving 69 reasons every 15 minutes, by the paper's count, why Alberta was not part of British Columbia.

September 22 was Calgary, Alberta, Day and exposition officials made doubly sure that the signs were correct. Yakima Valley Day was also celebrated with an abundance of apples. But there was sad news out of Minnesota: Governor John Johnson, who had visited the A-Y-P earlier, had died unexpectedly after a stomach operation.

COMFORT AND SORROW

September 23 was Walla Walla Day, and many came to see the unveiling of a statue of Dr. Marcus Whitman, one of the Northwest's earliest pioneers. The plaster cast was located near the Education Building and was a replica of a bronze statue that was later installed at Whitman College.

Hundreds of Walla Walla residents arrived by train to celebrate, and before traveling to the fairgrounds they probably wandered a few blocks over from King Street Station to check out a new luxurious comfort station that opened that day in Pioneer Place. Located underground below an ornate glass and iron pergola, the restrooms

had marble stalls, brass fixtures, white-tiled walls, and terrazzo floors. The men's and women's rooms each had an anteroom with oak chairs and a shoeshine stand.

City officials had hoped the comfort station would be open before the fair, but work was still going on in September, and the official opening wouldn't occur until January. But with President Taft arriving at the end of month, Seattle wanted to at least have it partially functional in the hopes of getting some good press.

On Friday, September 24, a terrible accident occurred near the fairgrounds. A Seattle Electric Company streetcar jumped the tracks and slammed into three concession buildings across the street from the main entrance. One person was killed and 55 were injured. Some of the more badly injured passengers were carried into nearby businesses and homes, while others were taken by roller-chairs and rickshaws to the exposition's Emergency Hospital.

LANGUAGE AND LIVESTOCK

Saturday was Esperanto Day for practitioners of the constructed language who hoped to one day see it become the "universal tongue." Esperanto was introduced in 1887 as a flexible language that might serve to foster international understanding. Those who spoke the language were excited to come to the fair and meet others they could converse with. But non-Esperantists were probably wondering what they were hearing when greeted with *"Saluton!"* or *"Pardonpetas, Kie estas la necesejo?"*

Over the weekend, work was completed on 18 new buildings at the south end of the fairgrounds for the big stockyard and poultry show that opened on Monday, September 26. Each building was 50 feet wide, and if laid end to end would have stretched almost a mile. Even with that much space, the A-Y-P still had to rent a garage on 23rd Avenue for overflow exhibits.

Described as the largest aggregation of purebred livestock ever assembled in the West, the show contained some 700 cattle, 300 horses, 700 sheep, and 350 swine. More than 5,000 birds were entered in the poultry show. Judging lasted almost two weeks, and on the first day alone thousands of people viewed the animals.

The largest individual cattle exhibit belonged to Seattle real-estate developer and model-farm owner James Clise, who displayed 33 head of Willowmoor Ayrshires. From Bowling Green, Missouri, came the country's largest mule, weighing in at 2,160 pounds. John Cubbey of Tacoma showed off his 900-pound swine.

ABOVE RIGHT: Grand Prize ribbon; **BELOW:** An elaborate arch erected at 2nd Avenue and Madison Street in downtown Seattle welcomed President Taft.

TAFT AND BRYAN

During the last few weeks of the A-Y-P, the fairgrounds were visited by the two men who had battled for the presidency a year earlier: William Howard Taft, a Republican from Ohio, and William Jennings Bryan, a Nebraska Democrat.

When President Theodore Roosevelt honored his promise to not run for a third term, he convinced his fellow Republicans to nominate Taft, his secretary of war. A rather large man with a genial smile, Taft ran as a progressive candidate wrapped in the mantle of his mentor. Bryan had already lost two presidential elections, against William McKinley in 1896 and 1900, but he still had popular support within the Democratic Party.

Businessmen supported Taft, but Bryan failed to secure the support of labor. Although Taft won the election by a comfortable margin, he was only in office for one term. In 1912, Theodore Roosevelt broke from the GOP, splitting the ticket. Woodrow Wilson eventually won decisively, and Taft suffered the single worst defeat in American history for an incumbent President seeking re-election.

PREPARING FOR THE PRESIDENT

During the week, a stronger military presence was noted around the city. Four companies of the First Infantry arrived in town in preparation for a visit from President William Howard Taft. Seven years earlier, President William McKinley had been assassinated while attending the Pan-American Exposition in Buffalo, New York, and no one wanted to see history repeat itself. The infantry would police the fair during Taft's visit, along with Seattle police officers and A-Y-P guards.

September 29 at the fair was Port Angeles Day and Washington Creamery Association Day. It was also Roycroft Day, honoring Elbert Hubbard's Roycrofters, a worker's community founded in 1897 to produce Arts and Crafts furniture, metalwork, and other objects by hand, and to advocate the Arts and Crafts philosophy that valued handcrafted over machine-made objects. But most exhibitors that day were sprucing up their buildings and booths to impress the president.

Just after midnight, President Taft's train pulled into King Street Station in downtown Seattle. He greeted the crowd and was whisked off to a brief reception at the Rainier Club before arriving at the Washington Hotel at 2 a.m. Another large crowd was on hand, and Taft was brought in through the women's entrance, which was guarded by Secret Service men. Just as he stepped into the elevator, he paused and told the guards to wait. Taft had heard the yells of some Yale men in the men's grill, and ran over to join them in some college cheers before going off to bed.

TOURING WITH TAFT

The next morning, Taft and his aide, Captain Archibald Butt, were ready to go by 9:15. They arrived by automobile at the A-Y-P at 9:45 and were driven directly onto the fairgrounds. The crowds were huge, and Taft waved to the throngs from the steps of the auditorium before reviewing a parade of all nations that marched past. At 10:30, he began his tour of some of the buildings, moving between them by car.

The plan had been to have the president view only a few exhibits, but Taft was interested in seeing as much as he could and led everyone around at a rapid pace. In the Alaska Building he tried his hand at panning for gold, and also got to inspect the treasure cage. At one point he was handed two gold nuggets, which he accepted and then handed to Captain Butt to hold for him. Throughout the tour Taft received all sorts of gifts, ranging from the largest apple in the Yakima exhibit to a gold enameled Cloisonné vase from the Japan Building.

In the California Building, he downed a refreshing glass of orange juice and tasted the wares at an olive booth, leaving the pit as a souvenir for the manager. Since Sacramento, California, was celebrating its Special Day, 10 crates of grapes were sent to the president's rail car. Taft ended his morning tour at the New York Building,

President William Howard Taft (center left), A-Y-P President John Chilberg (center right), and A-Y-P Master of Ceremonies Josiah Collins (lower right) leave the New York Building.

WATER WOES

By July, the A-Y-P, was draining more than one million gallons of water a day from the city system, and as a result, water pressure was so low faucets sometimes ran dry elsewhere. Harry Bringhurst, city fire chief, said the low water pressure was a threat to fire protection. To ease the strain, exposition managers began pumping water in from Lake Washington to irrigate the fairgrounds.

What they didn't know was that lake water ended up in the pipelines used for drinking water at the A-Y-P. When health officials noted an increase in typhoid cases in September, the cause was undetermined. It wasn't until the A-Y-P ended and typhoid cases dropped off that the association became clear. By the end of 1909, 511 people — including about 200 A-Y-P visitors — had been sickened by the disease. Of these, 61 died. One-third of the dead were tourists.

The epidemic led to a better understanding of the connection between drinking water and typhoid, a fact water officials took into account during the construction of newer pipelines. The 1909 outbreak remains the last significant epidemic of typhoid in Seattle.

where he spoke at a luncheon. Afterwards he gave a speech in the Natural Amphitheatre where a group of children once again formed a "living flag."

In the afternoon the fairgrounds tour continued. At the Arctic Brotherhood Building, the president received a degree making him an honorary Arctic Brother. The only mishap during the day occurred when Taft was stung on the neck by a bee while traveling in his car.

After a quick trip to his hotel to freshen up, Taft returned to the fairgrounds that evening for a grand banquet held in the Washington State Building. In his address, Taft spoke of the importance of Washington's role in Pacific trade, and singled out Seattle as a great example of the "power of the people and the possibilities of development in the Northwest."

Taft Day was attended by 60,953 people, making it one of the most popular days of the fair. The next day, Taft took part in a parade in downtown Seattle, and was driven back to the fairgrounds to oversee the stock show. After reviewing a livestock parade in the stadium, he left for a round of golf at the Seattle Golf and Country Club, and then traveled on to Tacoma aboard a private yacht.

A total of 840,504 people visited the fair in September, bringing in $245,993.99 in gate receipts.

BABIES, BUCKEYES, AND BOOTLEGGERS

The fair was winding down now, even though it still had a half-month to run. There were fewer Special Days, but still many events designed to draw people in. On October 2, close to 1,500 youngsters participated in a baby show in the auditorium. President Chilberg tried to give a speech but was drowned out by wails, cries, and shrieks from the small contestants. Prizes were awarded for the prettiest baby, the

ABOVE: William Jennings Bryan addresses the crowd in the A-Y-P amphitheatre; BOTTOM: Poster advertising William Jennings Bryan Day.

Yet another Children's Day was held on October 9, and every youngster under the age of 12 got in free. It was also the last day of the livestock show, and the boys and girls got to pet the lambs, calves, and piglets. One lucky girl, 10-year-old Margaret Atherton Jenkins, won a Shetland pony. When her name was announced at the parade grounds, she ran to the central stand as fast as she could while a crowd of thousands cheered her on.

Scandal broke out a week before the fair closed when every gate-keeper and admission inspector was fired due to rumors that they were stealing money. One man was seen pocketing a 50-cent piece given to him at the gate, and the others were deemed guilty by association. After an investigation, the charges were found to be bogus, and the men got their jobs back one day before the fair closed.

THE COMMON MAN

The fair welcomed its final famous visitor when William Jennings Bryan, who ran against Taft in the 1908 election, showed up on October 12.

While touring the exposition Bryan visited the Walla Walla exhibit, where a young woman pinned a ribbon on his lapel reading, "What Walla Walla Wants Is You." Later, during a luncheon at the New York Building, Bryan noticed that the people seated near him were sharing a joke. He asked President Chilberg why everyone was laughing, and Chilberg replied, "The joke is on you, Mr. Bryan. Our state penal institution is located at Walla Walla and the ribbon you wear intimates you're wanted there." Bryan took off the badge.

He gave speeches in the amphitheatre that afternoon and evening that were very well attended. In his evening speech Bryan criticized the Taft Administration and Republicans for an hour and a half. Afterwards, he and his wife, Mary, attended a reception in the Washington State Building.

FINAL DAYS

On October 13, hundreds of collegians wandered the grounds in rolled-up baggy, trousers, shouting "Sis-Boom-Ah" at University of Washington Day festivities. Great fun was made of the new crop of freshmen, who were made to parade down the Pay Streak with their shirt tails out. At one point, some of the downtrodden "freshies" were tossed into Geyser Basin, and its new moniker, "Frosh Pond," was born.

On the night of October 14, the wives of the Washington state commissioners held a banquet in the New York Building for the A-Y-P hostesses, thanking the women who had looked after the exposition's social side and served as den mothers in exposition buildings during the last four and half months. Many of the hostesses got up to speak, telling of their experiences and what they had gained.

California Building hostess Amanda Wiggins noted, "I believe that when we pass out the gates, every one of us will be a stronger and a more capable woman. Our duties have sometimes been arduous, sometimes tedious — there may have even been some

unpleasantness — but all these are overshadowed by all that has been beautiful."

The next night Governor Hay and members of the Washington state commission hosted a farewell reception and ball in the Washington State Building for exposition officials. It was the last social event at the A-Y-P

GOOD NIGHT AND FAREWELL

October 16, the final day of the exposition, was Hurrah Day, and although its intent was to cheer the monumental effort that had gone into creating and operating the fair, the event proved somber and bittersweet.

Beginning at 2:30 in the afternoon, Dad Wagner's A-Y-P Band serenaded the buildings, moving from one to the next throughout the afternoon. Sobs were heard in many of the buildings after the musicians had departed. As they passed through the streets, admirers shouted "Goodbye boys! God Bless You!"

On the steps of the Fine Arts Building, the band was met by Director of Ceremonies Josiah Collins, who presented the director with a gold medal. When the band reached the Government Building,

ABOVE: Ohio Day commemorative ribbon; **BELOW:** The Washington State Building was perfect for dancing; **OPPOSITE PAGE:** A-Y-P buildings such as the European Building were breathtakingly illuminated at night.

the flag was hauled down while the band played "Taps." The sound of a 21-gun salute boomed from Lake Union. The Igorrotes sang "My Country 'Tis of Thee." The crowd cheered, and the doors to the Government Building closed for the last time.

There were still a few hours left before the final ceremonies. Some people wandered the grounds; others took in Pay Streak amusements for the last time. Around 11 p.m., a crowd of about 15,000 people, led by Wagner's band, marched their way towards the amphitheatre. Many of them blew tin horns, but by the time they were seated, silence filled the air. It was only when Josiah Collins introduced President Chilberg that everyone stood up and cheered.

Chilberg told of the honor he had turning the first spade of earth at this very spot on June 1, 1907. He mentioned the promises that were made that the fair would be ready by June 1, 1909, and that it would end promptly at midnight on October 16, 1909. He continued, "I approach this duty with some feeling on my part, for there is something of sadness to realize that a bane of duty and pleasure should come to a close."

He thanked the countries and states that participated in the exposition. He thanked the city of Seattle, and also his own executive staff. He thanked Alaska, and wished it well.

He paused, looked at his watch, and in a voice thick with emotion said, "The fair is at an end."

Chilberg turned to the podium and flipped a switch, extinguishing all of the lights on the fairgrounds. In the darkness, a lone bugler played "Taps." In the darkness, thousands of voices choked through tears and sang a chorus from "Auld Lang Syne." In the darkness, they sat.

And when it was all over, the lights came back on and everyone broke into a rousing cheer that rolled on and on for 10 long minutes.

RIGHT: Aerial view from the tethered balloon; INSET: Pin-back A-Y-P button.

A FAIR TO REMEMBER

The A-Y-P Exposition turns a profit, but falls short (at least right away) of some of its organizers' grander dreams. The fair is memorable for its success in showing the bounties of Washington, Alaska, Canada, Japan, Hawaii, and the Philippines to the world. It also is remembered for bringing visitors from far and wide to Seattle, and for proving to Seattleites what their own civic determination can accomplish. The A-Y-P leaves a physical imprint on the city that is still visible and provides the inspiration for Seattle's second world's fair, the Century 21 Exposition of 1962.

The fair was over. Seattle may have paused to recognize it, slept a little later on Sunday morning, October 17. Almost immediately, though, attention shifted to counting up the profit.

During the Alaska-Yukon-Pacific Exposition's four-and-a-half-month run, total attendance was 3,740,551, and gate receipts topped out at $1,092,366.34.

The fair was over, but just as they had paid to watch the buildings rise, fair-lovers wistfully watched many of those buildings fall.

ABOVE: Quilt made from commemorative satin ribbons collected during the A-Y-P;
OPPOSITE PAGE: The A-Y-P Auditorium Building was renamed Meany Hall and served generations of students before earthquake damage in 1965 forced its demolition.

They could also enjoy some of the exhibits before these were packed up and shipped out. Over the next six weeks, exposition officials charged half-price admissions during daylight hours, so folks could wander around the fairgrounds as the A-Y-P slowly faded from sight.

PACKING UP, PULLING DOWN

The Pay Streak was the first to go. Within days, showmen broke down their booths, packed up their tents, disassembled rides, gathered weary performers, and moved on to the next carnival, fair, or boardwalk they could find. Small displays disappeared quickly from the exposition buildings, but more elaborate exhibits, such as those in the Government Building, required careful handling and an orderly process, which took more time.

ABOVE: The dinner that marked the formal dissolution of the A-Y-P Exposition Company featured a model of the Court of Honor crafted in sugar; **OPPOSITE PAGE, TOP RIGHT:** The Burke Museum, 2008; **OPPOSITE PAGE, BOTTOM LEFT:** The A-Y-P Exposition executive board presented John Chilberg with a huge silver chalice in appreciation for his faithful and efficient services.

By the end of the year, most buildings that university regents had not chosen for preservation were empty or being demolished. By spring 1910 they were almost gone. The nightly glow of the thousands of lightbulbs was now replaced by the lucent ambience of Halley's Comet overhead.

The buildings planned for permanent use by the University of Washington were already occupied by students and professors, who dragged their Bunsen burners and flasks into the Fine Arts Building — now their Chemistry Building — and attended engineering lectures in what used to be the Machinery Building — now their Engineering Hall. Other A-Y-P buildings that were saved were shored up and put into service.

The beautifully manicured exposition grounds, about which so many column inches of newspaper ink had been spilled, took on an apocalyptic appearance, chewed up by wrecking crews and dotted with decaying buildings. So hasty was the demolition that water lines were severed. Geyser Basin's plumbing began to leak. The new plantings the university put in to camouflage the mess before the 1910 Commencement Exercises were ineffectual.

In 1910, the Seattle Parks Department purchased 2,400 benches from the exposition for $1,000. The department was offered a herd of six camels from the Streets of Cairo concession, but declined.

SHARING THE WEALTH

On June 26, 1911, the A-Y-P Executive Committee met for the last time, to dissolve the Exposition Company and to recommend disbursement of funds on hand. After the business meeting, the men dined around a centerpiece almost as spectacular as the fair itself. A massive model of the buildings surrounding the Court of Honor was sculpted in sugar, down to the smallest detail. The entire tableau measured 10 by 14 feet, with the Government Building reaching three feet into the air.

Unlike previous expositions, the A-Y-P had money left over after stockholders received their final dividends. Of the $14,488 on hand, $366 went to the Seaman's Institute. The balance went to the Anti-Tuberculosis League of King County.

As successful as the A-Y-P was, dreams of widespread development and a statewide real-estate boom never materialized. Washington may have caught the nation's eye, but very few who traveled to enjoy the fair decided to stay. In Seattle, building starts proceeded at a relatively slow pace.

Back on campus, student enrollment climbed, but it was not until 1916 that the state Legislature allotted funds for new university buildings. When in 1915 Seattle architects Bebb & Gould (successor firm to Bebb & Mendel) were commissioned to create a building plan

EMMONS COLLECTION

George Emmons spent much of his U.S. Naval career in Alaska where he collected artifacts from Alaskan tribes, which he lent, donated, and sold to museums around the country. Exposition organizers asked Emmons to display part of his collection, consisting of about 1,800 objects mostly from the Tlingit Tribe of southeastern Alaska, in the Alaska Building.

After the fair, the Washington State Museum, now known as the Burke Museum of Natural History, moved into the California State Building. The university's regents raised funds, primarily through private donations, to purchase the Emmons collection, greatly expanding the museum's holdings and establishing a focus on Tlingit art that continues today.

for the University of Washington, they kept the Olmsted's A-Y-P orientation. Arctic Circle, by then beloved as Frosh Pond, became a nucleus from which the campus radiated.

PASSAGES

As many A-Y-P buildings faded into memory, so did the men whose grit had brought the fair into being. Godfrey Chealander, whose dream of showcasing Alaska's wonders had set A-Y-P into motion, moved from Alaska to Snohomish County and continued his retail operations there. In 1930 he moved south, and died in Los Angeles in 1953.

John Chilberg, whose steady attention to detail kept the fair on track, focused once again on his duties at the Scandinavian-American Bank in Seattle. In the 1920s, he fell on hard times, including an indictment on charges of financial impropriety, of which he was acquitted. After declaring bankruptcy he moved to California, where he died in 1954.

He taught up until the day he died in 1935.

The Washington State Museum benefited greatly from the A-Y-P. Besides gaining an important new collection that was displayed at the fair — the Emmons Collection of Tlingit artifacts — the museum used a variety of A-Y-P buildings over the years as it continued to grow. After a few years in the California Building, the museum moved to the Forestry Building, and after that building's demolition, settled into the Washington State Building. In 1964, the institution — now called the Thomas Burke Memorial Washington State Museum — opened a new building on the north campus.

Ira Nadeau, who had traveled the country promoting the A-Y-P and was present at almost every major ceremony during the summer of 1909, went to back to selling insurance. He died in 1930. Lake Nadeau in eastern King County was named in his honor.

John C. Olmsted, whose ground plan was integral to the fair-going experience, went on to design the Capitol Lake and preliminary plans for the Capitol campus in Olympia. He died in 1920.

Soon after his resignation, Director of Exploitation Henry Reed dropped his claim for extra compensation and moved back to Portland. In 1919 he directed the Portland Rose Festival and then became vice president of the city's planning commission. In his later years he was deeply involved with the Oregon Historical Society, up until his death in 1947.

Charles Wappenstein regained his job as Seattle Chief of Police when Hiram Gill was elected mayor in 1910. Within a year, Gill was recalled owing to corruption involving the police department, and Chief Wappenstein eventually ended up in the state penitentiary. After his release, he led a quiet life until his death in 1931.

Defying all odds, daredevil aeronaut J. C. "Bud" Mars lived to the ripe old age of 68. He trained pilots during World War I, built an airport in New York, and settled down as a businessman until his death in Los Angeles in 1944.

Edmond Meany remained a fixture on the University of Washington campus as a well-loved professor, historian, and mountaineer. The A-Y-P Auditorium was renamed Meany Hall in his honor in 1914, and in 1929, he donated his extensive collection of historical books, photographs, and documents to the university.

On January 3, 1959, Alaska became the 49th state. Columbia Eneutseak, who as Miss Columbia had personified the word Eskimo for an adoring public and had been the darling of the A-Y-P, died eight months later.

FROM A-Y-P TO CENTURY 21

By the 1950s, most of the people who were involved in creating the 1909 Alaska-Yukon-Pacific Exposition had died. Of the millions of people who attended the fair, many who were still around and remembered it fondly had experienced it as children. One of these was Al Rochester, who at age 14 had visited the A-Y-P almost every day.

By 1955, Rochester was a Seattle City councilman. Remembering the successes and joys of the A-Y-P, he began bandying about the idea of a second world's fair to commemorate the first. Initially, his idea met with mixed response, but Rochester kept pushing. Before long, he convinced enough people and work soon began on the Century 21 Exposition, set to open in 1962.

ABOVE: Sunkist used its A-Y-P diploma as a label on wooden crates of lemons; **OPPOSITE PAGE:** Century 21 Exposition proposed design by John Graham & Company.

An aerial view of the University of Washington campus in 1959, 50 years after the fair, reveals that John Olmsted's A-Y-P ground plan continues to influence the site's built and landscaped environments.

This new world's fair focused on such themes as science and space travel, and while everyone was thinking about jet-packs and bubble cars, the 50th anniversary of the A-Y-P became an afterthought. A small luncheon was hosted by the Seattle Historical Society, and the Ford Motor Company sponsored a cross-country auto rally to coincide with the Century 21 groundbreaking ceremonies. This time every car was a Ford, which assured the firm a victory.

Nevertheless, the links to the past were in place. Al Rochester served as executive director of the Washington State World's Fair Commission, and Henry Broderick, who in 1909 was the youngest

trustee of the Alaska-Yukon-Pacific Exposition, bridged the gap and became a trustee of Century 21.

A-Y-P Executive Director John Chilberg's widow, Anna, the fair's unofficial first lady, whose support behind the scenes had facilitated so many social occasions, received an invitation from Al Rochester to attend Seattle's 1962 World's Fair. Anna Chilberg wrote back, "This Exposition (Century 21) is so much bigger and of wider scope than A-Y-P.... How I wish my husband could have been here to experience the delight of another exposition in Seattle."

As with the first fair, the second exposition was a rousing success.

Besides providing Seattle with icons like the Space Needle and the monorail, it signified to the rest of the world that Washington was ready to help the nation move forward into the future.

SURVIVORS

In 1984, the University of Washington celebrated the 75th anniversary of the A-Y-P, focusing on the tremendous legacy of the fairgrounds. Although only a few of the original A-Y-P buildings remained, the campus still retained much of John C. Olmsted's plan.

A parade of vintage automobiles drove through the campus, along the curving roads Olmsted had planned. A coffee reception was held in the Burke Museum for anyone who had attended the exposition. One special guest was Alice McWilliams, aged 99, a 1910 graduate whose years on campus had dovetailed with the fair.

Few people at the celebration thought about the fair's built legacy, but it was there, hidden in plain sight. The Architecture Hall revealed its exposition roots most readily, still as graceful and imposing as it had been as the Fine Arts Pavilion. Modest Cunningham Hall across Stevens Way (the fair's Alaska Avenue) was once again spotlighting and serving women, as it had as the Woman's Building during the A-Y-P. The Michigan Club was still there just east of the Husky Union Building, the stunning Forestry Building's long-ago replacement. Of simple design but sturdily constructed, Michigan formed the kernel at the center of the university's Physical Plant Office Building.

MARKING A CENTENNIAL

A century after fairgoers first entered the exposition grounds, many of the dreams embodied by the fair are now reality. The region has grown in stature as a major hub of Pacific Rim trade and Seattle remains the state's gateway. Over time, the city developed into a metropolis well beyond what fair planners had hoped for. Newcomers mixed with pioneer descendants and the region became fertile ground for new ideas and innovations

The auto age that began with the mass production of Henry Ford's Model T connected urban, suburban, and rural communities but over-reliance on the internal combustion engine brought problems of its own. Washingtonians now look for other ways to get from place to place.

Though Bud Mars's airship bounced perilously over the exposition, air travel found its wings. Planes crossed countries and oceans, rockets shot off into space, and Seattle became synonymous with air transportation.

Suffragists used the fair to win the vote, and Washington voters have since elected many women to fill key political roles. Women's participation in the fair was mostly defined along then-expected lines of gender, but after a century men and women have pushed closer to a balance of equality.

Finally, fairgoers of 1909 would find the way the world communicates unrecognizable. Postcards written at the fair arrived home days later and moving images took weeks or even months to be seen by the rest of the world. If the fair were held today any visitor could share news, photos, or video within seconds.

Although the fair has passed from memory into history, its legacies remain. Perhaps most prominent is the framework of the fairgrounds, which is still more or less in place. Visitors to the campus can still follow its gentle curves, look out at Mount Rainier, and sense the presence and grandeur of the Alaska-Yukon-Pacific Exposition.

A bronze plaque commemorating the fair is located at the foot of Rainier Vista, a quiet reminder to University of Washington students of a major chapter in campus history.

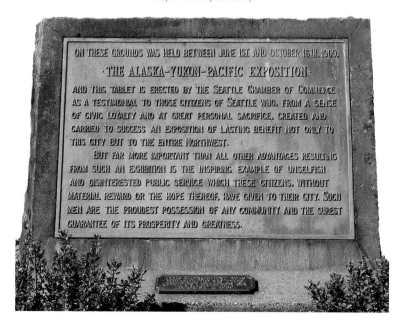

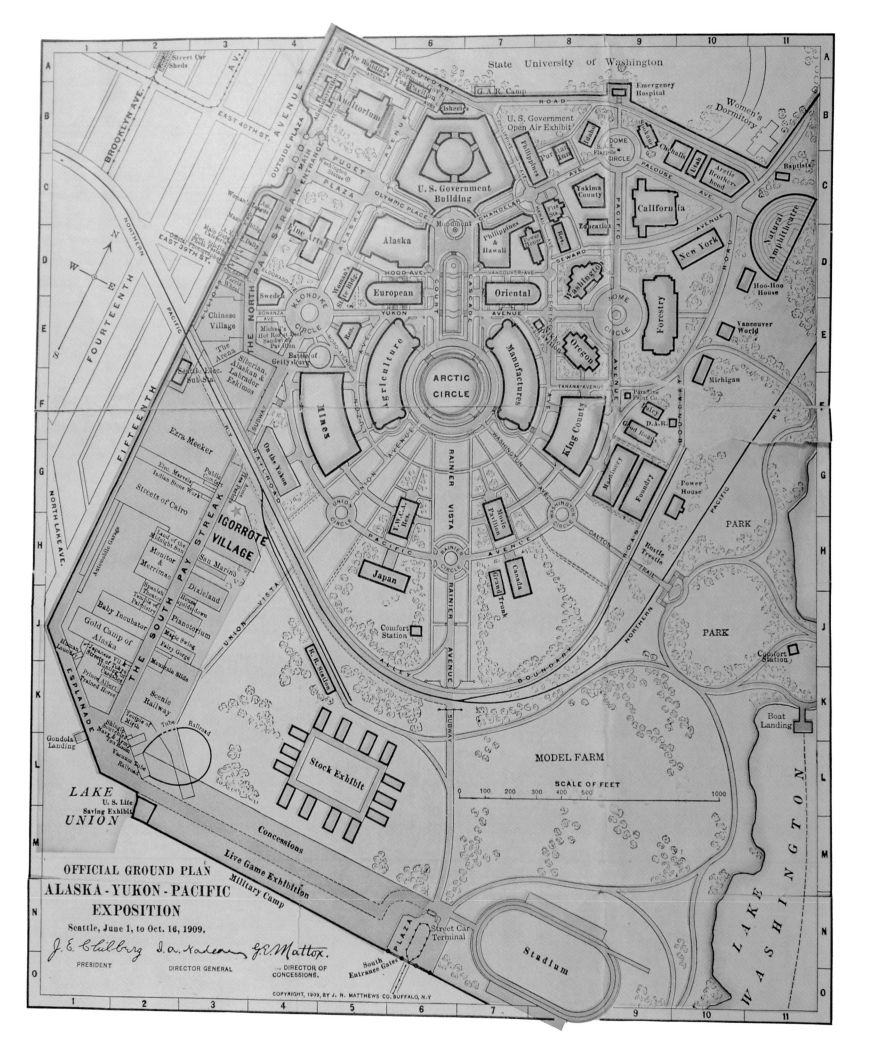

OFFICIAL GROUND PLAN
ALASKA - YUKON - PACIFIC EXPOSITION

Seattle, June 1, to Oct. 16, 1909.

J. E. Chilberg
PRESIDENT

I. A. Nadeau
DIRECTOR GENERAL

G. E. Mattox.
DIRECTOR OF CONCESSIONS.

The Alaska Building was a commanding structure that covered 36,000 square feet of land. This was the Northern Empire's first building in any exposition. Its exhibits showcased the tremendous resources that the territory had to offer, not the least of which was gold. One of the more eye-catching displays featured more than $1 million in gold nuggets, dust, and ingots inside a heavily fortified case. At the end of each day, the entire cage was lowered through the floor to an underground vault accessible only by tunnel.

Much of Alaska's wildlife was on display, either as taxidermy or in the form of fur pelts. Hungry visitors enjoyed the fish-canning exhibit, where a free dainty lunch was handed out, made from a different salmon recipe every day. Other exhibits included information about the territory's timber, whaling, mining, and burgeoning petroleum industries.

Steamship and railroad companies were well-represented, and many of these organizations urged people to travel north, hopefully to buy land or set up a business. Another exhibit highlight was a large collection of artwork, most notably by Native women.

The Alaska Building was demolished after the fair.

ARCTIC BROTHERHOOD BUILDING

Architect: Eben Sankey & Axel Edelsvord

Funded by Arctic Brotherhood

On site now: Communications Building

The Arctic Brotherhood Building was the first building on the A-Y-P grounds built by a fraternal organization. Designed as a log cabin similar to homes in Alaska, the structure had two floors, the second of which was large meeting hall with a massive fireplace made of clinker brick. The walls of this room were covered with displays of tools and utensils both

of miners and of Alaska Natives.

The Arctic Brotherhood was formed during the Klondike Gold Rush to protect the rights of miners, but by 1909, the group was more involved in the fight for Alaska self-governance. The group donated the building to the University of Washington, and it was used as a men's building and later the YMCA building until it was torn down in 1929.

AUDITORIUM BUILDING

Architect: Howard & Galloway

Funded by State of Washington

On site now: George Washington Statue plaza northwest of Meany Hall

Constructed of wood, with concrete and brick exterior walls, the Auditorium Building was an important venue for many concerts, speeches, and other formal gatherings during the A-Y-P. It seated 2,500 people. The main floor contained a stage/platform and seating. Wide stairways led from each side of the lobby to the balcony. Since the Auditorium was located near the A-Y-P Exposition's main entrance that emptied onto 15th Avenue, patrons exiting the Auditorium had easy access to streetcars.

After the fair the Auditorium was re-christened Meany Hall in honor of beloved University of Washington professor Edmond

Meany. It was remodeled 1925 and served the university community until structural damage received in the 1965 earthquake forced its demolition.

CALIFORNIA BUILDING

Architect: Sellon & Hemmings

Funded by State of California

On site now: Communications Building

The California Building, designed in Spanish Mission style, was a larger replica of California's building at the Lewis and Clark Exposition. It had a large central gallery area with two three-story wings and an 80-by-80-foot skylight. At the center of the building stood an enormous fruit pavilion featuring lions made of peaches, an elephant crafted of walnuts, an almond cow, and a raisin bear. Other displays highlighted the state's gems, minerals, salt and borax industries, and silk-manufacturing process from cocoon to fabric.

A working model of a 24-mule team and a 400-foot panorama showing California's bounty were popular features. Each of the state's 58 counties sent a display. The back of the building faced Lake Washington and featured a wide porch overlooking a garden of flowers and shrubs that were native to California.

California offered the building to the University of Washington, but evidently the university declined. It was demolished following the fair.

CANADA BUILDING

Architect: Not Available

Funded by Canadian government

On site now: Mueller Hall and area just north of Mueller Hall

The British Empire supplied the Dominion of Canada exhibits, some of which had been featured at the 1908 Franco-British Exposition in London. A display of grasses and of some 400 varieties of flowers demonstrated that the Canadian Yukon was more than a frozen land of ice and snow. Another display featured taxidermied examples of wild animals that lived in Canada. Many varieties of apples arranged in heaps, crates, bottles, and on glass pedestals formed another display. Klondike-mined examples of quartz, copper, silver, gold, and lead were featured, and an auditorium provided the

setting for illustrated lectures documenting the Gold Rush, from George Carmack's *Eureka!* on Bonanza Creek to 1909's most modern mining methods.

The building was demolished after the fair.

CHEHALIS COUNTY BUILDING

Architect: possibly Frank Allen or someone identified in clippings as "Architect Reed"

Funded by Chehalis County (note: in 1915 the county name was changed to Grays Harbor)

On site now: Skagit Lane between Miller Hall and Communications Building

The Chehalis County Building featured an elaborate frieze above its main entrance that depicted the county's main industries —

TOP: Canada Building; **ABOVE LEFT:** California Building; **RIGHT:** Chehalis County Building.

lumber, livestock, dairy, and farming. The interior was furnished entirely in native woods of Chehalis County, highly polished to accent the grains. It featured an office and retiring rooms.

Lumber mills and farm products dominated the exhibits, but the region's burgeoning fishing industry was also on display. Various women's clubs displayed their handiwork, and there was also a fine showcase of Indian artifacts. The Chehalis County Building was demolished after the fair.

DAIRY EXHIBIT BUILDING AND MODEL DAIRY BARN

Architect: Saunders & Lawton

Funded by State of Washington

On site now: Loew Hall

Dairying was one of Washington's chief industries in 1909, and the Dairy Exhibit and Model Dairy Barn introduced modern scientific methods of milk production to many dairying fairgoers. Eight cows lived in the scrupulously clean Model Dairy Barn. The barn and its attached milk house boasted the very latest in sanitary features, and scientific records of the cows' intake and output were maintained. One set of stalls was

constructed of concrete with steel stanchions, and another set was built completely of wood. Shelton Machinery Company made all of the machinery.

The milk house was equipped with boiler, steamer, bottle-washer, separator, and a Reid milk cooler. The milk the cows produced was sold at The Firs, the YWCA's A-Y-P restaurant.

After the fair the barn was used as living quarters, then until 1923 as the Carpenter Shop. It then became the Mason and Utilities Shop. In 1963 it became a lunchroom and locker room. The Creamery Building became the Carpentry Shop after the fair, then the Pipe and Machine Shop. The Building was destroyed by fire on April 1, 1961.

EDUCATION BUILDING

Architect: Saunders & Lawton

Funded by State of Washington

On site now: Open area Southeast of Allen Library

The Education Building hosted a model classroom, in session daily, and an ongoing Domestic Science (meal preparation)

demonstration given by girls from Olympia High School. These girls provided meals for many VIP receptions, held in a dining room within the Education Building. Boys demonstrated carpentry in an adjoining room. Large glass cases and exhibit areas throughout the building were filled with the work of schoolchildren from counties across the state.

After the fair the Education Building served as the university's Department of Journalism and as classroom space. It was demolished in 1917.

TOP: Education Building; BOTTOM: Dairy Exhibit Building.

EMERGENCY HOSPITAL

Architect: Howard & Galloway

Funded by A-Y-P Exposition Company

On site now: middle of quad between Miller Hall and Raitt Hall

The building was two stories with a basement, of frame construction finished with plaster. Facilities included a sterilizing room and a surgery, a diet kitchen, an office for medical director Dr. C. M. Rininger, two six-bed wards, three private rooms that could be used as wards if necessary, and living quarters for the medical staff. This could have been a useful building for the university to retain, but it was poorly constructed, with a wooden foundation, and its basement took in water even during the exposition. It was sited at the northern border of the fairgrounds, and once the A-Y-P was over the university deemed it too close to other buildings, and razed it.

EUROPEAN/FOREIGN BUILDING

Architect: Schack & Huntington, Howard & Galloway supervising

Funded by A-Y-P Exposition Company

On site now: Quaternary Research Center and C7 Parking Area

The European/Foreign Building — also called the Foreign Palace — was first intended to be used as the Fisheries Building, which was later constructed in back of the Government Building. The Foreign Palace was of French renaissance design, and was similar in appearance to the Oriental Palace, which was located directly across the Court of Honor.

The building contained exhibits from England, France, Germany, Spain, Holland, Sweden, Denmark, Norway, Russia, and Hungary. Included were artwork, ceramics, jewelry, textiles, food, and many articles manufactured in European countries. The structure was torn down after the fair ended.

FINE ARTS BUILDING

Architect: Howard & Galloway

Funded by State of Washington

On site now: Building survives.

The Fine Arts Building, just north of the main gate of the exposition, exhibited paintings, photographs, and sculptures gathered from around the country by Director of Fine Arts G. L. Berg, who was also the Secretary of the Washington State Art Association, one of the precursors of the Seattle Art Museum. Two of the eight main galleries displayed examples of great European art including works by El Greco, Van Dyk, Jean-Baptiste-Camille Corot, Jean-Francois Millet, as well as English

TOP LEFT: Emergency Hospital; TOP RIGHT: Fine Arts Building; BOTTOM: European/Foreign Building

portraitists and French Impressionists. The remaining six galleries displayed works by American painters, including a John Singer Sargent (*Mrs. Fiske Warren*) and a number of landscapes. Two small rooms featured an exhibit of Edward Curtis's photography and the atrium featured a small display of sculptures. A critic from *Scribner's Magazine*, the artist Ernest C. Peixotto, noted that the exhibition had a "decidedly uneven merit," but forgave that because of Seattle's remoteness. He decried the random display of the pieces, however, as a fault of all exhibitions at the time. Museums and galleries were just beginning to hang artwork according to a scheme intended to educate the audience.

John Galen Howard, of Howard & Galloway, designed the building in the Iconic style, featuring four columns at the front of the building. It housed three floors of rooms and an auditorium.

The Board of Regents had determined that this building would be the University's Chemistry Building after the fair, and it was designed accordingly. It served that purpose until 1937 when it was remodeled for the Physiology and Architecture departments. Since 1946 it has been used for architecture alone. A major retrofit of the building in 1987 renovated the interior, essentially building a concrete structure within the frame of the old building for seismic safety. The Department of Construction Management of the College of Architecture and design studios for the Department of Architecture are now located in the building, along with a coffee shop that has the distinction of being the campus's first non–Husky Union Building coffee shop, opened in the early 1960s.

FIRE STATION

Architect: Howard & Galloway

Funded by A-Y-P Exposition Company

On site now: area north of Suzzallo/Allen Libraries and south of Gowen Hall

The Fire Station was a two-story structure that housed horses, two engines, a hook and ladder truck, and two hose carts. The upper story contained a private office for the chief and engineers, as well as quarters for the men. The station was manned around the clock during the fair so that firefighters could respond to a call on the grounds at any moment, day or night. The building was razed after the fair.

FORESTRY BUILDING

Architect: Saunders & Lawton

Funded by State of Washington

On site now: Husky Union Building

Fir logs with bark left intact provided the Forestry Building with dramatically memorable decorative elements and also served its function. Felled in Hazel, near Arlington, in Snohomish County in October 1908, these logs formed 124 columns that were each four-and-a-half feet in diameter and 37 feet high. Each massive column weighed 50,000 pounds and contained sufficient board feet to build a five-room cottage. All told, some 2.5 million feet of lumber were utilized to create the Forestry Building. Spiral staircases at each end reached up to a balcony exhibit space.

A display showed visitors timber at every stage of the manufacturing process, from felled tree to finished flooring, paneling, mill work, and decorative elements — potent proof of Washington's timber resources. A giant set

TOP: Forestry Building; **BOTTOM:** Fire Station.

of wooden dice, a display of cedar shingles, exhibits documenting Washington's history, and an anti-tuberculosis exhibit were displayed. The south half of the main floor contained a fish hatchery, preserved fish in specimen jars, live fish in aquariums, and live seals. At the south end of the massive hall was a mountain with streams flowing past growing sod, ferns, and animals preserved by taxidermy. Behind the Forestry Building was the so-called "Big Stick": a 156-foot piece of milled timber that could be viewed from below. Nearby was a shorter 87-foot pole that could be straddled; it made a popular subject for camera-wielding fairgoers.

After the fair it served as the University's forestry building. Several years later the collections of the Burke Museum were moved to the Forestry Building, but the discovery of dry rot in 1923 forced its closure and, in 1930, its demolition.

GOOD ROADS BUILDING AND EXHIBIT
Architect: Bebb & Mendel
Funded by State of Washington
On site now: Loew Hall

Of wood construction, the Good Roads Building held exhibits designed to educate the public about the need for better highways. The

automobile was steadily eclipsing the horse as a means of transport. The Washington Good Roads Association, formed in 1899, managed the building during the fair. Exhibits included road-building materials, methods of construction, short stretches of every kind of road, and stereopticon lectures documenting existing roads and road-building efforts underway at the time, as well as stereopticon views documenting resources, industries, and scenery around the state. A 300-seat auditorium accommodated these lectures. On the main floor the Good Roads Building featured a model of the quarry at Deception Pass on Fidalgo Island. At the time, most of the rock used to prepare roads in Western Washington came from this quarry.

After the fair the building was used for a variety of purposes, eventually becoming the Air Force ROTC Building. It burned to the ground in April 1961.

HAWAII BUILDING
Architect: Howard & Galloway
Funded by United States government

The Hawaii Building was a large structure, located prominently near the Government Building. Exhibits were designed to acquaint the world with the "new" Hawaii.

Native artifacts were in abundance, but the importance of Hawaii's role as a U.S. territory, not a "possession," was heavily stressed. This was the first time that the Territory of Hawaii had ever taken a prominent part in any exposition.

A great concrete water tank, 60 feet in length, ran through the center of the building and provided visitors with an overview of the islands in miniature. Prominence was given to the location and strategic importance of Pearl Harbor, where work had just begun on what was termed an "impregnable naval base." Elsewhere on the map, the volcano of Kilauea emitted a plume of smoke at regular intervals.

Visitors enjoyed a daily series of motion pictures depicting various aspects of island life. Other educational films from around the nation were shown as well. After each viewing, people enjoyed slices of tasty pineapple served up at polished koa wood tables.

The Hawaii Building was demolished after the fair.

HOO-HOO HOUSE
Architect: Ellsworth Storey
Funded by Hoo-Hoo Society
On site now: University of Washington Club

TOP: Hawaii Building; **BOTTOM:** Good Roads Building.

Idaho's Mission-style building featured displays illustrating the state's mining industry, including rocks, ores, minerals, and photographs of mining operations. Educational displays emphasized the handwork of the state's schoolchildren, and mounted photographs documented classroom life. The Idaho Building's interior was illuminated by skylights and left unadorned, giving it a warehouse-like appearance that the flags and bunting hung from beams did little to disguise. The building was razed following the fair.

JAPAN BUILDING

Architect: N. Ikeda

Funded by Japanese government

On site now: Anderson Hall

The Hoo-Hoo House was built by the Hoo-Hoo, a lumbermen's fraternity, and was designed in a bungalow style. Atop the roof on each gable were ornamental black cats, and in front of the building were two large cat statues with green electric eyes that shone brightly at night. Black cats were the adopted mascots of the Hoo-Hoos, and the number 9 played an important part in Hoo-Hoo ritual, owing to a cat's legendary "nine lives."

from the entrance.

The Hoo-Hoos donated the building to the University of Washington, and after the fair it was used as the Faculty Club until 1959, when it was torn down. The Faculty Club has since been renamed to the University of Washington Club, and its building is in the same location.

IDAHO BUILDING

Architect: James A. Fennell, Wayland & Fennell

Funded by State of Idaho

On site now: Quad just north of Smith Hall

Nestled in a grove of fir trees, the Japan Building was styled after traditional Japanese architecture and stood in exotic relief against the fair's prevailing neoclassical style. It was painted red. Exhibits included teas, silks, porcelain, wood, lacquerware, kimonos, Yuzen dyeing, musical instruments, Mikimoto cultured pearls, and displays of consumables including canned codfish, menthol oil, dried ginger, marin, sake, peanuts, and peanut oil. Glass cases lined all interior walls, with further exhibit cases in the center of the room. Japan,

Besides being a gathering place for visiting lumbermen, the Hoo-Hoo House was also used for banquets, receptions, parties, and even weddings. The interior was filled with sturdy, handcrafted, wooden furniture and the walls were fully paneled. An enormous fireplace, 10 feet across and six-and-a-half-feet deep, was on the east side of the clubroom, directly across

TOP: Hoo-Hoo House; ABOVE LEFT: Idaho Building; ABOVE: Japan Building.

having emerged victorious from the Russo-Japanese War of 1905, and in the process of annexing Korea, had achieved political equality with the West and become the strongest imperialist power in Asia. The Japanese government displayed charts, maps, and model warships that boasted Japan's modern shipbuilding program and the Mikado's army and navy. A display of photographs of Kyoto, Tokyo, and other cities educated fairgoers about Japan. A cloisonné vase, worth $5,000 and said to be the largest of its kind, was also featured. Fairgoers who trekked to the Formosa Tea House at the northern end of the fairgrounds could sample tea grown on the island (now Taiwan), Japan's second largest export after silk.

The building was demolished after the fair.

KING COUNTY BUILDING

Architect: Not Available

Funded by King County

On site now: Aerospace Research Building and open area surrounding it

The King County Building was a two-story structure, built in simple Renaissance style. Its outdoor garden produced crates of strawberries that were distributed to visitors. Exhibit space inside was free to King County producers. The building also housed the offices of the Seattle Press Club, where much of the active newspaper work on the grounds took place.

The first floor contained a massive cyclorama that detailed the resources and development of King County. A smaller exhibit illustrated Seattle's regrade work, using an illusion by which a large hill disappeared from view, displaced by an image of skyscrapers and graded streets. The Seattle Public Schools conducted an ongoing manual-training exhibit where classes of boys practicing bench work alternated with classes of girls practicing cooking.

The second floor showcased more than 150 county manufacturers, featuring products that ranged from furniture and appliances to artificial limbs and soap. The King County Building was demolished after the fair.

LIFE SAVING STATION

Architect: Not Available

Funded by United States government

On site now: Fisheries Center Pond

Located at the foot of the Pay Streak on the shores of Lake Union, the Life Saving Station housed members of the United States Life-Saving Service, who gave daily demonstrations of their work. The structure consisted of an office building, a light tower, and a storage area for their fleet of three life-saving vessels. A model ship's mast was located offshore, and was connected to the light tower with a breeches buoy line.

TOP: Life Saving Station; **BOTTOM LEFT:** King County Building; **BOTTOM RIGHT:** Machinery Building.

A large seating area was located directly to the southeast, so that crowds could watch the men at work. Each day, members of the crew took a dunking out in the water, and were "rescued" by other members of the service. Two of the lifeboats were self-righting, and demonstrations were given of their capabilities in adverse conditions.

After the fair, the building was used as the Varsity Crew House. It was torn down in 1920.

MACHINERY BUILDING

Architect: Howard & Galloway

Funded by State of Washington

On site now: Mechanical Engineering Building

Constructed by the Westlake Corporation of St. Louis using its own heavy machinery brought west by rail, the Machinery Building was designed to serve the Mechanical and Engineering departments after the fair. It housed functional machines of every sort, including milling machinery, band saws, and machines for manufacture of wire ropes and cables. Two popular exhibits were the timber-testing plant, at which wood was tested to the breaking point, and the stone-testing plant, at which stone was tested to the crushing point. A model foundry stood nearby.

The building was demolished in 1957.

MANUFACTURES BUILDING

Architect: Somervell & Coté, Howard & Galloway supervising

Funded by A-Y-P Exposition Company

On site now: space east of Drumheller Fountain in front of Guggenheim Hall

The Manufactures Building was of French renaissance design and curved around the east side of Geyser Basin. It covered 60,000

square feet of ground and contained numerous displays of manufactured articles. Inventors who wanted to promote their inventions (for example a Snore Silencer) had booths. Female fairgoers flocked to the Singer sewing machine booth, and music lovers without the skill to play coveted player pianos.

Many exhibits were educational and showed how products were made. Weaving machines manufactured silk embroideries. Knives and scissors were manufactured, as were burnt-leather goods, furniture, and carpets. A model printing plant was used to print sheet music. The building also housed an extensive arts and crafts exhibit. Organizations with a message rather than a product, like the Woman's Christian Temperance Union, also had booths in the Manufactures Building

After the fair, the building was used for campus purposes until 1918, when it was torn down.

MICHIGAN CLUB BUILDING

Architect: James C. Teague

Funded by Michigan State Society

On site now: Building survives as Physical Plant Office Building

TOP: Michigan Club Building; **BOTTOM:** Manufactures Building.

When the state of Michigan declined to appropriate funds for a building at the A-Y-P, the local Michigan Club funded one. It served as the Michigan Club's headquarters during the fair. Of frame construction with a stucco exterior, the building was later shingled, then sided. It was remodeled in 1940, enlarged in 1957, and (remarkably for such a humble structure) still survives.

MINES BUILDING

Architect: Schack & Huntington, Howard & Galloway supervising

Funded by A-Y-P Exposition Company

On site now: Benson Hall

The Mines Building was planned along the Court of Honor, the main buildings that surrounded the cascades and geyser basin and were the focal point of the fair, but the building intended for it became the Oriental Palace. The Mines Building was instead located behind the Agriculture Building, and featured various aspects of mining industry in the Pacific Northwest.

Displays included large blocks of granite, sandstone, onyx, marble, and other minerals. Examples of clay were shown from every county in Washington. Metal mining was represented by more than 400 separate exhibits

from 39 mining camps. Numerous types of ore, crystals, and coal were on view.

Once a day, the Government Mines Rescue Service gave a demonstration on how injured miners were saved following gas leaks, rock falls, or explosions.

The Mines Building was demolished after the fair.

NEW YORK BUILDING

Architect: Clarence Luce

Funded by New York State

On site now: N-22 Parking Area directly across Stevens Way from Hall Health

The New York State Building was modeled after the Auburn, New York, home of former Governor William H. Seward. As Secretary of State under Abraham Lincoln, Seward negotiated the treaty with Russia that authorized the United States purchase of Alaska. The building was adapted especially for social gatherings, and after

the Washington State Building was disallowed for banquet use, New York ended up hosting most of the A-Y-P Exposition's important luncheons and dinners.

The building featured a women's reception room and men's reception room off the main hallway. Beyond that was a large banquet room that could easily seat more than a hundred people. Throughout the building were photographs and paintings depicting scenes in the Empire State. A private sitting room with full bedroom upstairs meant that the New York Building could house dignitaries overnight.

After the fair, the building was turned into the University of Washington President's Residence. During a remodel in 1920, all the porches and verandas surrounding the structure were torn down. After the president moved into a new residence in 1927, the structure became the Music Building. It was demolished in 1950.

OREGON BUILDING

Architect: D. C. Lewis

Funded by State of Oregon

On site now: west end of Seig Hall

Oregon's was the first state building erected. It was two stories high and topped by a large

TOP: New York Building; BOTTOM: Mines Building.

dome. A giant panoramic painting depicted scenic Oregon sites. Displays highlighted Oregon's forestry, mineral wealth, fishing industry, and bounteous fruit and vegetable production, including many heaps of grape clusters. In addition to exhibit halls the building featured a reception room, retiring rooms, and suites for the governor and commissioners. It also included a cold-storage plant where Oregon apples and possibly fruit from other exhibit buildings could be stored prior to display.

After the fair it was used briefly as the Law Building, then razed in 1917.

ORIENTAL BUILDING

Architect: Schack & Huntington, Howard & Galloway supervising
Funded by A-Y-P Exposition Company
On site now: Mary Gates Hall

The Oriental Building — also called the Oriental Palace — was first intended to be used as the Mines Building, which was later constructed southwest of the Agriculture Building. The Oriental Palace was of French renaissance design, and was similar in appearance to the European Building, which was located directly across the Court of Honor.

Exhibits in the building were mainly from Asian countries, although European countries were included due to limited space in the European Building. Nations represented included China, Korea, India, New Zealand, Italy, the Netherlands, Austria, Belgium, Serbia, Greece, Turkey, Egypt, Syria, and Persia. The structure was torn down after the fair.

PHILIPPINE BUILDING

Architect: Howard & Galloway
Funded by United States government
On site now: Front portion of Gowan Hall and Spokane Lane in front of it.

The contents of the Philippine Building were designed to show how Filipinos had "developed" during the decade since the Philippine Islands had come under America's control, as well as to highlight the islands' rich resources. Among the many items on display were Native handcrafts, a stack of guns surrendered during the Spanish American War, colored transparencies showing scenes of daily life, Philippine wood, hemp, and bamboo items, elaborate carvings, many items crafted out of mother of pearl, export products such as tobacco, hemp, and sugar, and several relief maps. The Philippine Building also featured full-sized dioramas depicting an Igorrote village and a Negrito village with mannequins bizarrely replicating the living tribespeople on display in the Igorrote Village concession on the Pay Streak.

After the fair the Philippine Building became the UW's Mines Rescue Building. It was razed in 1921.

TOP: Oriental Building; MIDDLE: Philippine Building; LEFT: Oregon Building.

POWER HOUSE

Architect: Howard & Galloway

Funded by State of Washington

On site now: Still exists with many additions

The A-Y-P Power House was intended to function as the University of Washington's permanent power plant after the fair. The boilers originally burned coal, but were later converted to burn oil and gas. A smoke stack was added in 1923, and was replaced in 1988. The Power House received additions in 1923, 1935, 1939, 1950, 1960, 1962, 1965, 1969, and 1978, and with these improvements it still services the university.

SPOKANE COUNTY BUILDING

Architect: Preusse & Zittel

Funded by Spokane County

On site now: Miller Hall

The Spokane Building was built in the style of Spanish mission architecture, topped by four central towers, with four smaller towers at each corner of the structure. The main entrance featured a cozy veranda, furnished with rockers, wicker chairs, and benches.

Inside, the arched ceiling was painted flat black and was decorated with a series of friezes made entirely out of seeds, grain, and grasses. Each image was modeled after actual photographs depicting scenes from Spokane County. Large portraits of Theodore Roosevelt and President Taft, done in the same way, hung on the wall, as did the state seal and an image of George Washington.

Half of the building was reserved for a large resting lounge, filled with comfortable furniture and Spokane newspapers and promotional literature.

The Spokane Building was demolished after the fair.

SWEDISH BUILDING

Architect: Not Available

Funded by Swedish government

On site now: Guthrie Hall

The Swedish Building drew many visitors eager to see Henry Hammond Ahl's painting, *The Shadow of the Cross*, an unfinished depiction of Christ that reportedly emanated a mysterious glow when viewed in darkness. The Swedish Building featured an auditorium, reception rooms, and a library that stocked copies of every Swedish newspaper published in Sweden and in America.

The Swedish Building was demolished after the fair.

UNITED STATES GOVERNMENT BUILDING

Architect: Howard & Galloway, Supervising Architects

John Knox Taylor, Supervising Architect of the Treasury

Funded by United States government

On site now: Red Square (Central Plaza Garage)

TOP: Power House; **BOTTOM:** Spokane County Building.

TOP: Swedish Building;
BOTTOM: United States Government Building.

The enormous Government Building was the crowning building at the A-Y-P, a font of knowledge, wisdom, and patriotism whose presence gave the fair substantial ballast.

The Departments of State, Treasury, War, Justice, Post Office, Navy, Interior, Agriculture, and Commerce and Labor all had display space in the Government Building, as did the Smithsonian Institution and National Museum. A mint struck commemorative medals, which were then sold by private concessionaires. A guard force protected the exhibits around the clock, at night carrying side-arms. The building was open from 9 to 5:30 Monday through Saturday and closed on Sunday. A fisheries exhibit occupied a separate building that was linked to the main Government Building by an enclosed passage. Among the hundreds of thousands of items displayed in the Government Building were a desk on which a rough draft of the Declaration of Independence was written, George Washington's eyeglasses, various congressional war and peace medals, facsimiles of many historic documents, a knife that had cut more than $5 billion worth of currency over its time in use, melting furnaces and machinery for coining money, a printing press in operation, an assay office, model ships, marine hospital equipment, a model operating room with full-sized wax figures, an army wagon used in Sherman's march to the sea, guns, portraits, letters signed by presidents and other statesmen, a functioning model post office, a lithographic printing press on which three-color maps of Seattle were printed, the original Northern Pacific Railroad (later renamed Railway) mortgage secured by its federal land grant, a rural schools exhibit, two large panoramas representing Yellowstone Falls and Crater lake, a large glass weather map, 650 specimens of commercial apple varieties, working plans for Pacific Coast model farms, a refrigerator case stocked with slaughtered animals demonstrating the importance of rigid inspection during cattle slaughter, samples of tissue infected with tuberculosis, giant models of crop-damaging insects, a model of an irrigated farm, a public roads exhibit, many lighthouse lenses and an operational lighthouse, model locomotives, relics from Catholic missions in California, a large Mormon Church exhibit, and a large exhibit documenting the history of photography.

The Government Building was demolished after the fair.

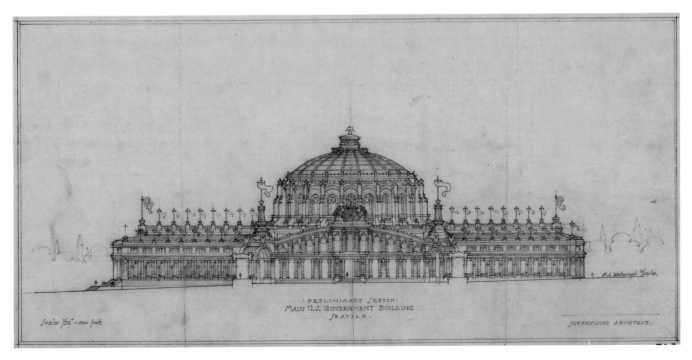

UTAH BUILDING

Architect: Not Available

Funded by State of Utah

On site now: area northwest of Miller Hall

The Utah Building was modeled after traditional Hopi pueblo dwellings with wooden ladders and artificial *vigas* (round supporting roof beams that project out from the structure), in this case serving a decorative rather than functional purpose. Displays included Utah schoolchildren's handcrafts and test papers, paintings and historical objects, salt from Great Salt Lake, examples of items produced in Utah, and other examples of industrious activity supporting Utah's motto, "Busy All The Time." Special copper and silver medallions imprinted with the Utah state seal were sold in the Utah Building. The building was demolished after the fair.

WASHINGTON STATE BUILDING

Architect: Bebb & Mendel

Funded by State of Washington

On site now: open area Southeast of Allen Library and north of Seig Hall

The Washington State Building was the official home of the exposition and the citizens of the state, and boasted a generous open floor space ideal for large receptions, banquets, and dancing. Beginning in July the general public was invited to weekly dances in this space, which was also used regularly by many Special Day groups for dances and receptions. All important visitors to the fair, including President William Howard Taft, were entertained in this building. The building's interior was finished in rich, fine style, demonstrating how beautiful Washington's timber could look in its most processed form. The Washington State A-Y-P commissioners had executive offices on the first floor, and the second floor housed men's and women's drawing rooms and rest rooms and a smaller reception room that fairgoers also could use as an inside place to bring their lunches.

After the fair it was remodeled and used as the University of Washington Library, and after 1927 as the Washington State Museum. Part of the building was demolished in 1961, the rest on November 2, 1988.

WASHINGTON WOMAN'S BUILDING

Architect: Saunders & Lawton

Funded by State of Washington

On site now: Building survives, but UW plans to relocate it some time before December 2009 to make way for the new Molecular Engineering Building.

The Washington Woman's Building (also called the Woman's State Building or simply the Woman's Building) was created at the behest of Spokane resident Lena Erwin Allen representing the 90 clubs that made up the

TOP: Utah Building; **BOTTOM:** Washington State Building.

Washington State Federation of Women's Clubs. Members of these clubs successfully lobbied state legislators for funding, and University of Washington alumnae and women students raised money for furnishings. During construction in November 1908, *Alaska-Yukon Magazine* called the Woman's Building "practically permanent." The Woman's Building was used during the A-Y-P Exposition for teas and receptions, as a display space for women's creative work, to publicize women's achievements, and to serve female fairgoers. The second floor featured a free nursery/kindergarten staffed with two trained nurses and stocked with toys. A total of 2,007 children were cared for in this nursery, presumably freeing their mothers to better enjoy the fair. A small retiring room where mothers could rest and nurse their babies was much appreciated and in nearly constant use.

After the fair the Woman's Building was used briefly for its intended post-fair purpose as a center for women's activities on campus. In 1916 the structure was appropriated to house an experimental mining station. In 1927 it became the Chemistry Annex and in 1937 the home of Army ROTC. In 1969 it became the Atmospheric Sciences Annex. Not until 1983 was it re-designated to serve women, at which time it was renamed Imogen Cunningham Hall. As of 2008 the humble Woman's Building, and its much grander neighbor, the Fine Arts Building (now the Architecture Building), are the sole surviving public buildings erected for the A-Y-P Exposition.

YAKIMA COUNTY BUILDING

Architect: Henry F. O. Pohl

Funded by Yakima County

On site now: space north of Allen Library

The Yakima County Building was a two-story rectangular structure, ornamented with cases and boxes filled with plants furnished by the women's clubs and school children of North Yakima. Outside gardens were watered using an irrigation system of flumes and laterals, similar to farmland in Yakima County.

Inside, the smell of fruit was overwhelming. Large displays of cherries, apricots, peaches, apples, and all kinds of berries filled the first floor. Other farm products such as potatoes, hay, and alfalfa were also on view. Upstairs, visitors could examine ore from mines, and products like milled flour, canned fruit, and cruets of cider vinegar. A large relief map of the county was on display, as was a collection of baskets,

blankets, and clothing made by Yakama Indians.

Weary walkers enjoyed the men's smoking room, filled with easy chairs and settees, and the women's lounge, which included writing desks.

The Yakima County Building was demolished after the fair.

OTHER BUILDINGS included the American Women's League Building, Baptist Building, Daughters of the American Revolution Building, Fisheries Building, Foundry Building, Grand Trunk Railway, Masonic Building, Michel's Hot Roast Beef Pavilion, Music Pavilion, Natural Amphitheatre, Puritan Inn, Stadium, Stock Exhibit, Vancouver World Building, and Pay Streak concessions.

TOP: Yakima County Building;
BOTTOM: Washington Woman's Building.

GLIMPSES OF OLMSTED

CAMPUS
OF THE
STATE UNIVERSITY OF WASHINGTON

ALASKA·YUKON·PACIFIC·EXPOSITION
SEATTLE, WASHINGTON
1909
PLAN OF GROUNDS AND BUILDINGS
SCALE—ONE INCH EQUALS EIGHTY FEET
OLMSTED·BROTHERS
LANDSCAPE·ARCHITECTS
HOWARD·GALLOWAY
SUPERVISING·ARCHITECTS

LEFT: John C. Olmsted's axial plan for the grounds with three vistas captured views of Lake Washington, Lake Union, and Mt. Rainier. A century later Rainier Vista continues as a defining element of the University of Washington campus.

ABOVE CENTER: Fairgoers enjoyed strolling through the formal gardens located at the top of the three vistas radiating out from Geyser Basin. (Lake Union Vista shows on the right.) The east and west divisions of the garden had 5,000 roses in beds with 80,000 English daisies followed by dwarf phlox. The central Rainier Vista section of 50,000 flowering plants included poppies, phlox, delphinium, dianthus, and begonia providing colors from white to pink, orange, purple, yellow, red, and rich blue.

CLOCKWISE FROM TOP LEFT: The Cascades water feature under construction in 1908; The rustic trestle bridge that spanned the railroad tracks east of the central fairgrounds offered visitors a connection to the natural shorelands; Pathways along Lake Washington on the east edge of the fairgrounds purposely retained the shoreline's natural beauty; Fairgoers enjoyed the contrast between the Beaux Arts glamour of the fairground buildings and the rustic restful qualities inherent in Olmsted's design; A graceful swath of irises softens the formality of Washington Circle lily pond on Lake Washington Vista.

Denny Party lands at Alki Point on November 13, 1851.

Washington Territory is established on March 2, 1853.

Territorial University opens in downtown Seattle on November 4, 1861.

U.S. Senate ratifies purchase of Alaska from Russia on April 9, 1867.

Seattle is incorporated on December 2, 1869.

Clara McCarty becomes the first person to graduate from the University of Washington in July 1876.

Washington becomes a state on November 11, 1889.

First Great Northern train arrives in Seattle on January 7, 1893.

World's Columbian Exposition opens in Chicago on May 1, 1893.

Panic of 1893 begins on May 5, 1893.

University of Washington moves from downtown Seattle to its present campus in 1895.

Gold prospectors begin traveling north to Alaska in April 1895.

William D. Wood, a Republican, is appointed mayor of Seattle on April 6, 1896.

Klondike Gold Rush begins on July 17, 1897.

William D. Wood resigns as mayor of Seattle to look for gold in the Klondike in July 1897.

Thomas D. Humes, a Republican, is appointed mayor of Seattle on November 19, 1897.

Pan-American Exposition opens in Buffalo, New York, on May 1, 1901.

TOP: Gold seekers at Chilkoot Pass, Alaska, 1897; MIDDLE LEFT: Luggage tag; MIDDLE RIGHT: Hotel Savoy brochure; BOTTOM: Seattle brochure distributed at A-Y-P; OPPOSITE PAGE: A-Y-P coupon tickets were signed by the user and non-transferable.

Louisiana Purchase Exposition opens in St. Louis, Missouri, on April 30, 1904.

Albert Mead, a Republican, is elected governor on November 8, 1904.

Godfrey Chealander first suggests Alaskan exposition to be held in Seattle in May 1905.

Lewis and Clark Centennial Exposition opens in Portland, Oregon, on June 1, 1905.

Alaska-Yukon Exposition Company is incorporated on May 8, 1906.

King Street Station opens in Seattle, supporting both the Great Northern and Northern Pacific railroads, on May 10, 1906.

Alaska-Yukon Exposition officers are elected with John Chilberg as president on May 19, 1906.

Edmond Meany and the A-Y-P Committee request the Board of Regents to allow A-Y-P Exposition to be held on University of Washington grounds on June 16, 1906.

University of Washington campus is selected as the exposition site on June 22, 1906.

The word "Pacific" is added to the exposition name on July 6, 1906.

Henry E. Reed is appointed director of exploitation for the exposition on August 13, 1906.

In one day the people of Seattle subscribe to $650,000 worth of A-Y-P Exposition stock on October 2, 1906.

Lease between University of Washington and the A-Y-P Exposition for use of the grounds begins on October 2, 1906, and runs through January 1, 1910.

Organized publicity for the exposition starts in newspapers and magazines nationwide on October 5, 1906.

Preliminary plan of exposition is adopted on November 5, 1906.

President Roosevelt recommends A-Y-P Exposition in his message to Congress on December 3, 1906.

Exposition capital stock is increased to $800,000 on December 24, 1906.

Oregon Building site is selected on December 29, 1906.

Frank Allen is appointed A-Y-P director of works on December 31, 1906.

Seattle doubles in size by annexing six towns in 1907.

Washington Legislature appropriates $1 million for the exposition on February 1, 1907.

Oregon votes for a sum of $100,000 for building and exhibits on February 23, 1907.

U.S. Senate passes a $700,000 bill for participation in March 1907.

California appropriates $100,000 for participation on March 2, 1907.

Missouri appropriates $10,000 for participation on March 3, 1907.

Utah appropriates $2,000 for participation on March 19, 1907.

Pennsylvania appropriates $75,000 for participation on May 7, 1907.

Revised exposition plan is approved on May 17, 1907.

A-Y-P groundbreaking is attended by 15,000 on June 1, 1907.

Washington Governor Albert Mead convenes the first meeting of the Washington State Alaska-Yukon-Pacific Exposition Commission on June 1, 1907.

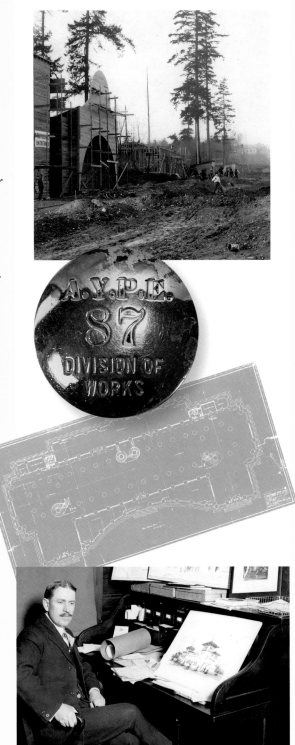

TOP: Grading crew levels site for Pay Streak, December 16, 1908; SECOND: Division of Works uniform button; THIRD: Forestry Building floor plan; BOTTOM: Director of Concessions A. W. Lewis.

Adelaide Hansom wins $500 in an A-Y-P logo design contest in July 1907.

Seattle annexes Lake Union shore lands on July 1, 1907.

Architects are employed to prepare plans for the Washington State Building and the Forestry Building on July 19, 1907.

Jamestown Exposition opens in Hampton Roads, Virginia, on April 26, 1907.

Executive commissioner is instructed on to urge county commissioners to levy taxes to prepare exhibits August 23, 1907.

Thomas Payne is elected secretary of the A-Y-P Exposition Commission on November 2, 1907.

Representatives of Seattle labor unions visit President Chilberg regarding the hiring of non-union men at reduced wages to construct A-Y-P buildings on December 20, 1907.

A-Y-P Exposition Commission meets in Olympia to confer with state institution heads on March 13, 1908.

Seattle annexes Lake Washington shore lands on March 21, 1908.

U. S. government appropriates $600,000 for exposition buildings and exhibits on May 23, 1908.

Final grading on the principal features is completed during the summer of 1908.

Newly appointed Federal Government Board of Managers meets for the first time on July 17, 1908.

Supervising Architect of the Treasury submits plan for A-Y-P Exposition Government Building on August 4, 1908.

Sydney Fischer, minister of agriculture at Ottawa, accepts the invitation to participate in the A-Y-P Exposition in August 1908.

A-Y-P grounds pre-fair admission charge is fixed at 10 cents on September 1, 1908.

Contract of $58,340 is let for the Washington State Building on September 16, 1908.

United States Department of State forwards invitations for participation to all foreign diplomatic officers of the United States on September 16, 1908.

Stockholders Day is held on September 18, 1908, and shareholders are invited to the grounds to see the progress being made.

Pre-fair grounds admission charges begin on September 20, 1908.

Contract is let for the Forestry Building on October 5, 1908.

Henry Reed resigns as director of exploitation on October 16, 1908, and James Wood replaces him.

Federal Government Board of Managers members meet with A-Y-P executive committee officers and tour the grounds on October 23, 1908.

William Taft is elected president on November 3, 1908.

Samuel Cosgrove, a Republican, is elected governor of Washington on November 3, 1908, but serves only one day before leaving office due to health reasons.

Lieutenant Governor Marion E. Hay, a Republican, is named acting governor on November 4, 1908.

First A-Y-P Fire Company goes into service on December 8, 1908.

TOP LEFT: Washington Governor Marion Hay; TOP RIGHT: Flags of countries comprising the International Union of the American Republics, A-Y-P; MIDDLE: First Olmsted Brothers' A-Y-P grounds plan; BOTTOM LEFT: Ferris Wheel; BOTTOM RIGHT: Seattle Chamber of Commerce brochure prepared for visiting dignitaries from California.

Edmond Meany is elected as an A-Y-P Exposition Commission trustee on January 11, 1909.

Seattle City Light installs ornamental street lighting in Seattle during the spring of 1909.

Exposition managers ask all residents of Seattle on February 7, 1909, to mail at least five letters to friends outside Washington encouraging them to attend the A-Y-P.

The Seattle Daily Times prints 100,000 copies of a 188-page issue on February 14, 1909, devoted almost entirely to promoting the A-Y-P, and sends 37,000 of these to cities beyond Seattle.

George Dickson is elected president of the A-Y-P Exposition Commission on February 15, 1909.

Anti-Tuberculosis League of King County is founded on February 15, 1909.

Two men are killed at a sewer cave-in near the A-Y-P grounds on February 23, 1909.

Work begins on moving a million bedding plants into place on exposition grounds on March 1, 1909.

Seattle and King County school children write letters to corresponding grade pupils in other schools on March 5, 1909, inviting them to attend the fair.

Route of transcontinental auto race is decided on March 13, 1909.

A-Y-P pre-fair admission charge is increased to 25 cents on March 15, 1909.

State Labor Commissioner reports that eight-hour workday rules are being violated at the fairgrounds on March 25, 1909.

Seattle and King County school children are admitted to the grounds for free on March 27, 1909, in thanks for their A-Y-P letter campaign.

Second A-Y-P Fire Company goes into service on May 7, 1909.

The Exposition Commission meets in Olympia on May 13, 1909, and agrees to add a Domestic Science and Manual Training department for the Education Building.

The Exposition publicity department wages a campaign to get as many "page stories" as possible into newspapers around the country on May 13, 1909.

The Federal Government Board of Managers members arrive in Seattle on May 17, 1909, to supervise final details and to participate in opening ceremonies.

Michigan Building is dedicated on May 22, 1909.

A-Y-P grounds are closed to the public on May 25, 1909, until opening day.

University of Washington graduation exercises are held in the Manufactures Building on May 31, 1909.

As midnight approaches, James Frederick Dawson supervises laying of final sod on May 31, 1909.

U.S. President Taft presses a telegraph key in Washington at 12:30 to open the fair on June 1, 1909.

Edmund Smith, inventor of a salmon-processing machine, is killed in an auto accident on the way to the exposition on June 1, 1909.

Bering Sea Day, Valley Day (Kent, Auburn, Puyallup, Sumner), and University of Washington Alumni Day are held on June 2, 1909.

TOP: Invitation to sit on Speaker's Platform on Opening Day; MIDDLE: Olympia High School domestic science and manual work demonstrators; BOTTOM LEFT: Welcoming pin for the Japanese naval ships Aso and Soya; BOTTOM MIDDLE: Vancouver, B.C., Daily World headquarters; BOTTOM RIGHT: A-Y-P Commemorative Spoon.

Military Day is held on June 3, 1909.

Japanese Navy Day is held on June 4, 1909.

Children's Day, Puget Sound Navy Yard Day, and Port Orchard Day are held on June 5, 1909.

Chicago Association of Commerce Day is held on June 7, 1909.

Washington Children's Home Society Day, Transcontinental Passenger Agents' Day, and Washington State Library Association Day are held on June 8, 1909.

Catholic Foresters' Day, Grocers' Day, Pioneer Association of the State of Washington Day, and Woman's Christian Temperance Union Flower Mission Day are held on June 9, 1909.

Yakima County Day is held on June 11, 1909.

Commercial Travelers' Day is held on June 12, 1909.

British Columbia Week starts and Daughters of the American Revolution Day, Sons of the American Revolution Day, Pullman Day, and Flag Day are held on June 14, 1909.

George Washington statue is unveiled on a temporary pedestal on June 14, 1909.

Order of the Eastern Star Day, Grand Lodge Free and Accepted Masons' Day, California Promotion Committee Day, and Pacific Coast Advertising Men Day are held on June 15, 1909.

Washington State Graduate Nurses' Association Day is held on June 16, 1909.

M. Robert Guggenheim, promoter of transcontinental auto race, is arrested for speeding in Seattle on June 17, 1909.

Inland Empire Week starts on June 21, 1909.

Royal Arcanum Day (Royal Masons) is held on June 23, 1909.

First transcontinental auto race ends in Seattle on June 23, 1909.

Washington State Federation of Women's Clubs Day and State Grand Army of the Republic Day are held on June 24, 1909.

Spokane Day is held on June 25, 1909.

King County Day, Davenport and Sprague Day, and Bankers Association Day are held on June 26, 1909.

Skagit Valley Week begins on June 28, 1909.

Kamloops Day is held on June 29, 1909.

Suffrage leaders from around the country arrive in Seattle by special train on June 29, 1909.

Cherry Day is held on July 1, 1909.

Railway Men Day, King County Day, Coal Miners' Day, and Lumbermen and Loggers' Day are held on July 3, 1909.

C. A. Beebe and Margaret Hall are married on the Pay Streak on July 3, 1909.

Pythian Week and Pacific County Week begin, and Polish Day, Ohio Society Day, Washington State Day, Baptist Young People's Union Day, and Valley Day (Kent, Auburn, Puyallup, Sumner) are held July 5, 1909.

Baptist Day is held on July 6, 1909.

Woman Suffrage Day and Pythian Day are held on July 7, 1909.

Pacific County Day, South Bend Day, Colfax Day, Billings Day, and Chehalis Day are held on July 8, 1909.

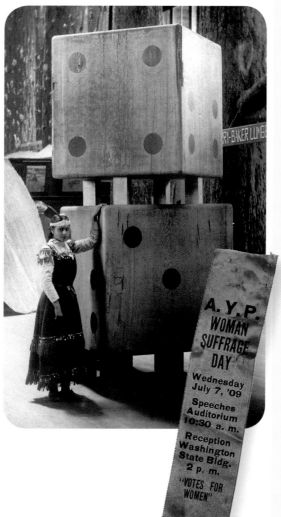

TOP LEFT: King County brochure; **TOP RIGHT:** Spokane pin-back button; **MIDDLE:** Giant wooden dice in Forestry Building; **BOTTOM:** Woman Suffrage Day ribbon.

Oregon Day and Pennsylvania Day are held on July 9, 1909.

Kansas Day, Sailors and Mariners Day, Americana or Innes' Day, and Sigma Chi Day are held on July 10, 1909.

Epworth League Day; Montana Day (unofficial); Pacific Coat Lumber Manufacturer's Day; Seattle Real Estate Association Day; and Yamhill County, Oregon, Day are held July 12, 1909.

Newberg, Oregon Day; Whatcom County Day; and Bellingham Day are held on July 13, 1909.

Pacific Coast Lumberman's Day, San Juan Day, National Council of Women Day, and Washington Press Day are held on July 14, 1909.

United Amateur Press Association Day; Eagles Day; Colorado Day; Sherman County, Oregon, Day; and Washington State Press Association Day are held on July 15, 1909.

Teachers' Day, Tacoma Day, Druggists' Day, and Washington Press Day are held on July 16, 1909.

A-Y-P officials shut down Klondike Dance Hall on the Pay Streak on July 16, 1909.

Washington State Dental Society Day and Astoria Day are held on July 17, 1909.

Cheyenne Bill's Wild West Show, featuring Tom Mix, opens at Madison Park on July 17, 1909.

San Bernardino Day and National Education Day are held on July 19, 1909.

National Editorial Association Day, Portland Day, Salem Day, and Baby Christening Day are held on July 20, 1909.

State Medical Association Day, Women's Press Club Day, and Hood River County Day are held on July 21, 1909.

Redmens' Day; Union, Oregon, Day; Benton, Oregon Day; and Butte and Anaconda Day are held on July 22, 1909.

Joseph Morhinway, a member of the Order of Red Men, is accidentally killed in a mock skirmish at the stadium on July 22, 1909.

Ancient Order of United Workmen Grand Lodge of Washington Day, Degree of Honor Day, and Fraternal Brotherhood Day are held on July 23, 1909.

Swedenborg Day and Delta Sigma Delta Day are held on July 24, 1909.

Santa Barbara and Ventura Day, San Luis Obispo and Paso Robles Day, and Brooklyn Day are held on July 26, 1909.

Union County Day, second Vancouver Day, Southern California Day, and Oklahoma and Indian Territory Day are held on July 27, 1909.

Woman's Christian Temperance Union Day; Baker City, Oregon, Day; Port Townsend Day; and Elks' Day are held on July 28, 1909.

Swedish Finnish Temperance Association Day, New Jersey Day, Delaware Day, National Union Day, Elks' Day, and West Virginia Day are held on July 29, 1909.

International Military Day is held on July 30, 1909.

Woman's Christian Temperance Union representatives issue national letter on July 30, 1909, advising their members not to attend the A-Y-P without a male escort and not to send young people to the fair alone.

Fairgoers climb and summit Mount Rainier and place at the peak an A-Y-P flag along

with a smaller "Votes For Women" flag attached to same staff on July 30, 1909.

Swedish Day is held on July 31, 1909.

Kentucky Day and New York Day are held on August 2, 1909.

Missouri Day, Exhibitors' Day, Minnesota Tricity Day (Duluth, Minneapolis, St. Paul), and Snohomish County Day are held on August 3, 1909.

James J. Hill statue is unveiled on August 3, 1909.

Woodsmen of the World Day, Women of Woodcraft Day, Olympia and Shelton Day, and Mississippi Day are held on August 4, 1909.

Alaska Children's Day is held on August 5, 1909.

Lewiston Day, Illinois Day, Alaska Womens' Day, Chehalis County Day, Sigma Nu Day, and National Hostesses' Association Day are held on August 6, 1909.

Indiana Day, Renton Day, Washington Rural Letter Carriers' Day, and Seattle Business College Day are held on August 7, 1909.

Los Angeles Day; and Pasadena, Santa Monica, Ocean Park, Whittier, and Venice Day are held on August 9, 1909.

Arizona Day; American Association of Titlemen Day; National Protective Legion Day; Vancouver, Washington, Day; and Association of Park Superintendents' Day are held on August 10, 1909.

Rossland, B.C., Day is held on August 11, 1909.

Iowa Day; Worcester, Massachusetts, Day; and Tucson, Arizona, Day are held on August 12, 1909.

TOP LEFT: Snohomish County Day ribbon; TOP RIGHT: Shelton booster button; THIRD: Music pavilion at night; FOURTH: A-Y-P season pass; BOTTOM: Washington State Commission Historical Exhibit Director badge.

Manila Day is held on August 13, 1909.

Visiting Knights of Columbus Day and Amateur Athletic Union Day are held on August 14, 1909.

Pennsylvania Day is held on August 16, 1909.

Toppenish Day, Great Falls Day, Nebraska Day, and Centralia Day are held on August 17, 1909.

German Day, Douglas County Day, and National G.A.R. Day are held on August 18, 1909.

Maccabees Day, International Improvement Club Day, and National Prison Congress Day are held on August 19, 1909.

Pay Streak Day, Theatrical Mechanics Association Day, and International Improvement Club Day are held on August 20, 1909.

Caledonian Day, Vancouver Arch Dedication Day, and Children's Day are held on August 21, 1909.

International Beauty Day and Congress of Educators of Indians Day are held on August 23, 1909.

Coeur D'Alene, Wallace, and Wardner, Idaho, Day; Acme Business College Day; and Dixie Day are held on August 24, 1909.

Mystic Shriners Day, Modern American Day, Utah Day, Hawaii Day, Governors' Day, and Chautauqua Day are held on August 25, 1909.

Maryland Day; Salt Lake City, Ogden, Provo and Logan Day; and Stanford University Day are held on August 26, 1909.

Welsh Eisteddfod Day, South Dakota Day, and Octogenarian Day are held on August 27, 1909.

TOP: Model of Mormon Tabernacle in Government Building; SECOND: Japan Day ribbon; THIRD LEFT: Arrival Arch erected in downtown Seattle by representatives from Vancouver, B.C.; THIRD RIGHT: Smith Day ribbon; BOTTOM: Loading riders into Vacuum Tube Railway.

Cactus Dahlia Day, Manufacturers' Day, and State Mining Day are held on August 28, 1909.

Norway Day is held on August 30, 1909.

Holland Day, Washington State Direct Legislation League Convention Day, and Michigan Day are held on August 31, 1909.

Eighteen-year-old Edna Clark from Bellingham falls dead at the exposition on August 31, 1909.

Wisconsin Day is held on September 1, 1909.

Okanogan Day and Smith Family Day are held on September 2, 1909.

Luther Burbank visits the A-Y-P on September 2, 1909.

Wenatchee Day and Pacific Coast Billposters and Distributors Association Day are held on September 3, 1909.

San Francisco Day, Japan Day, and Prince Rupert Day are held on September 4, 1909.

George Bech, composer of the official Seattle Day song, dies on September 5, 1909.

Seattle Day, Vashon Island Day, and Young Ladies Day are held on September 6, 1909.

Postmasters' Day is held on September 7, 1909.

Farmers' Day, International Language Day, and Klickitat County Day are held on September 8, 1909.

Gorham Company of New York completes design work on Henry Dosch's sketch for A-Y-P exhibitors' awards medals and exposition officials place an order for 8,000 on September 8, 1909.

California Day, Hoo-Hoo Day, Volunteer Firemen Day, Northwest Light & Power Association Day, and Raisin Day are held on September 9, 1909.

Seward Day and Washington State Fourth Class Postmaster's League Day are held on September 10, 1909.

Statue of William Seward is unveiled on September 10, 1909.

New England Day, United Spanish War Veterans' Day, King County Children's Day, and Santa Clara Valley Day are held on September 11, 1909.

Clarence Darrow visits the A-Y-P on September 12, 1909.

Montesano Day and China Day are held on September 13, 1909.

Ellensburg Day, Photographers Association of the Pacific Northwest Day, Vashon Island Day, and Boise Day are held on September 14, 1909.

Adams County Day and Foreign Consuls Day are held on September 15, 1909.

Igorrote child is born on exposition grounds on September 15, 1909, and is later named "President Taft."

Idaho Day is held on September 16, 1909.

Alameda County Day and Exhibitors' Day are held on September 18, 1909.

Nevada Day, Italian Day, Prince Edward Island Day, and Postmasters' Day are held on September 20, 1909.

Edmonton, Alberta, Day is held on September 21, 1909.

Yakima Valley Day; Calgary, Alberta, Day; and Blaine Day are held on September 22, 1909.

International Order of Odd Fellows Day, Walla Walla Day, and Anacortes Day are held on September 23, 1909.

Marcus Whitman statue is unveiled on September 23, 1909.

Underground comfort station opens in Seattle's Pioneer Place on September 23, 1909.

Streetcar crashes at A-Y-P entrance, killing one and injuring 55, on September 24, 1909.

King County Sunday School Day, Esperanto Day, American Music Society Day, and Cosmopolis Day are held on September 25, 1909.

National Funeral Directors' Association Day is held on September 27, 1909.

Lynden Day and Everson Day are held on September 28, 1909.

Port Angeles Day, Roycroft Day, and Washington Creamery Association Day are held on September 29, 1909.

President Taft arrives in Seattle on September 29, 1909.

Taft Day and Sacramento Day are held on September 30, 1909.

Ohio Day is held on October 5, 1909.

Apple Day is held on October 6, 1909.

Texas Day is held on October 7, 1909.

Ketchikan Day, Wrangell Day, and Children's Day are held on October 9, 1909.

Alaska Week begins and Stevens County Day and Fisherman's Day are held on October 11, 1909.

TOP LEFT: Idaho Day ribbon; **TOP MIDDLE:** San Diego Day ribbon; **TOP RIGHT:** Stevens County Day ribbon; **MIDDLE:** Guess-Your-Weight concession; **BOTTOM:** Carnation Milk advertising postcard.

William Jennings Bryan Day, Nevada Day, and Hotel Men's Day are held on October 12, 1909.

University of Washington Day is held on October 13, 1909.

Washington Publicity Day is held on October 15, 1909.

Closing Day and Hurrah Day are held on October 16, 1909.

A-Y-P fire companies are withdrawn and the station on the grounds is abandoned on December 6, 1909.

A-Y-P Exposition Commission adjourns on December 31, 1909.

A-Y-P Exposition Commission lease of the University of Washington grounds expires on January 1, 1910.

University District Improvement Club objects on January 8, 1910, to moving the Spokane Building to University Boulevard.

Nursery opens on five acres of A-Y-P grounds on January 8, 1910, to sell plants that the owner obtained from various exhibitors.

California Building is torn down in 1915.

Law Building (Oregon Building) is torn down in 1917.

Manufactures Building is torn down in 1918.

Music Pavilion, Armory (Oriental Building), and Varsity Crew House (Life Saving Station) are torn down in 1920.

Mines Rescue Building (Philippines Building) is torn down in 1921.

Gatzert Building (Masonic Building) is torn down in 1922.

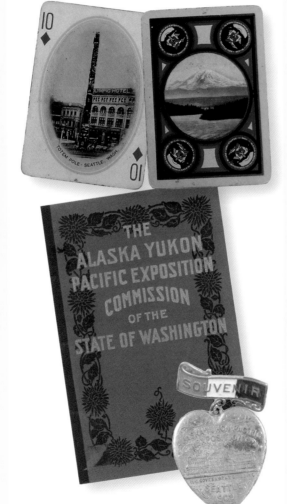

TOP: Shooting Gallery on the Pay Streak; SECOND: A-Y-P playing cards; THIRD: Cover of Washington State Commission final report; BOTTOM: U. S. Government Building souvenir pin.

Arctic Brotherhood Building is torn down in 1929.

Forestry Building is torn down in 1930.

Practice Cottage (Women's League Building) is torn down in 1946.

Music Building (New York Building) is torn down in 1950.

Engineering Hall (Machinery Building) is torn down in 1957.

Alaska becomes a state on January 3, 1959.

Faculty Club (Hoo-Hoo House) is torn down in 1959.

A-Y-P 50th Anniversary celebration is held on June 1, 1959.

Front portion of High Energy Physics Lab (Washington State Building) is torn down in 1961.

Air Force ROTC Building (Good Roads Building) burns to the ground on April 1, 1961.

Century 21 World's Fair opens in Seattle on April 21, 1962.

Meany Hall (Auditorium Building) is torn down following earthquake damage in 1965.

Washington Woman's Building is rededicated as Cunningham Hall on May 10, 1983.

A-Y-P 75th Anniversary celebration is held on June 1, 1984.

Remaining portion of High Energy Physics Lab (Washington State Building) is torn down on November 2, 1988.

A NOTE ON SOURCES

Frank Nowell's team of photographers poses with cameras and tripods in front of the
Official Photographer's Building on the north Pay Streak.

WE PORED THROUGH NUMEROUS PERIODICALS OF the day including
*The Seattle Daily Times, Seattle Post-Intelligencer, The New York Times, The
Seattle Star, The Billboard, Alaska-Yukon Magazine, The Christian Science
Monitor, The Yakima Herald, The Argus, The Interlaken, A-Y-P News,* and
the A-Y-P *Official Daily Program.*

We conducted archival research at the University of Washington
Libraries Special Collections, Washington State Historical Society,
Washington State Library, Oregon Historical Society, Seattle Public
Library Northwest Collection, Museum of History & Industry, Seattle
Municipal Archives, Whatcom Museum of History and Art, and the
Washington State Archives, Puget Sound Region.

We consulted the key contemporary publications documenting the
A-Y-P including The Secretary's Report of the Alaska-Yukon-Pacific
Exposition; The Report of the Alaska-Yukon-Pacific Exposition of the
State of Washington; The Alaska-Yukon-Pacific Exposition Directory;
Report of the United States Government Board of Managers, Alaska-

Yukon-Pacific Exposition, Seattle, Washington;
The Exhibits of the Smithsonian Institution and
United States National Museum at the Alaska-
Yukon-Pacific Exposition, Seattle, Washington,
1909; and New York at the Alaska-Yukon-Pacific
Exposition Seattle, Washington, June 1-October
16, 1909.

Valuable books on earlier expositions and
contemporary social issues include Jim Zwick's
*Inuit Entertainers in the United States from
the Chicago World's Fair through the Birth of
Hollywood,* Carl Abbot's *The Great Extravaganza:
Portland and the Lewis and Clark Exposition,*
Elana F. Fox's two-volume *Inside the World's
Fair of 1904: Exploring the Louisiana Purchase
Exposition,* Norman Bolotin and Christina
Laing's *The World's Columbian Exposition: The
Chicago World's Fair of 1893;* the anthology *Fair
Representations: World's Fairs and the Modern
World* edited by Robert W. Rydell and Nancy
Gwinn; Robert W. Rydell's *World of Fairs
The Century-of-Progress Expositions,* and most
importantly Rydell's *All the World's a Fair.*

We also benefited from two excellent master's theses: Veta R.
Schlimgen, "Defining Participation and Place: Women and the Seattle
World's Fairs of 1909 and 1962" (University of Washington, 2000), and
Barry J. McMahon, "Seattle's Commercial Aspirations as Expressed in
The Alaska-Yukon-Pacific Exposition" (Washington State University,
1960).

Finally, the University of Washington Libraries Special Collections
"Guide to the Frank H. Nowell Alaska Yukon Pacific Exposition
Photographs 1907-1909," processed by Solveig Ekenes, Laurel G. Evans,
Katie Maynard, Amy Lavare, and Roni Greenwood under the direction
and inspiration of Visual Materials Curator Nicolette Bromberg,
organizes and annotates one of A-Y-P's most important treasure troves
of original source materials: the nearly 1,000 images that constitute the
Frank Nowell A-Y-P collection. This guide was an invaluable resource
and greatly aided our research.

INDEX

IMAGE CREDITS

Collections (UW 197332, UW C0017, Campus Photographs).

P. 21.

Olmsted Brothers' 1904 University of Washington campus plan. Courtesy University of Washington Libraries Special Collections (UW 15724).

A-Y-P grounds prior to construction. Courtesy University of Washington Libraries Special Collections (AYP769, PH Coll. 757.5).

Brooklyn neighborhood (later University District). Courtesy University of Washington Libraries Special Collections (Asahel Curtis Collection, Cur263 and Cur266, A.Curtis 03190 and A. Curtis 03191).

Observatory. Courtesy University of Washington Libraries Special Collections (UW 6830, UW Campus Photographs, UW CO222).

P. 22.

Formal invitation. Courtesy University of Washington Libraries Special Collections (PAM 0150, Pacific Northwest Collection, T890 D9 A43 1908).

P. 23.

Jamestown Exposition logo. Courtesy History Ink.

P. 24.

Fine Arts Building. Courtesy University of Washington Libraries Special Collections (AYP159, Nowell x44).

Frank P. Allen, Jr. Courtesy University of Washington Libraries Special Collections (AYP369, UW 727.817).

P. 25.

Montlake ditch. Courtesy University of Washington Libraries Special Collections (SEA1880, UW 22087).

P. 26.

Adelaide Hanscom's logo in paint. Courtesy University of Washington Libraries Special Collections (27909z, PH Coll. 727.F154z).

Print. Courtesy University of Washington Libraries Special Collections (PAM 0150, detail).

Cloisonné. Courtesy Dan Kerlee.

Plaster. Courtesy Museum of History & Industry (1974.5868.9).

P. 27.

John Edward Chilberg breaks ground. Courtesy University of Washington

Libraries Special Collections (AYP1248, PH Coll. 727.3).

P. 28.

Construction workers and plasterers. Courtesy University of Washington Libraries Special Collections (AYP521, UW 26864).

P. 29.

Workers raise the flagpole. Courtesy University of Washington Libraries Special Collections (AYP490, Nowell x1243).

Exposition grounds were cleared of stumps. Courtesy University of Washington Libraries Special Collections (AYP1209, UW11729).

Manufactures Building nearing completion. Courtesy University of Washington Libraries Special Collections (27910z).

P. 30.

Formal gardens. Courtesy University of Washington Libraries Special Collections (AYP262, Nowell x2138).

John C. Olmsted. Courtesy of National Park Service, Frederick Law Olmsted National Historic Site and Friends of Seattle's Olmsted Parks.

James Frederick Dawson. Courtesy National Park Service, Frederick Law Olmsted National Historic Site and Friends of Seattle's Olmsted Parks (Olmsted Brothers A-Y-P Exposition Photo Album No. 7, Photo 2739-535, Nowell x1272).

P. 31.

Agriculture Building under construction. Courtesy University of Washington Libraries Special Collections (AYP508, UW 28043).

P. 32.

Spokane County marked their building's site. Courtesy University of Washington Libraries Special Collections (AYP1167, Nowell x176).

Groundbreaking ceremonies for the Swedish Building. Courtesy University of Washington Libraries Special Collections (AYP184, Nowell x1059).

P. 33.

Young women posed in living tableaux. Courtesy University of Washington Libraries Special Collections (AYP138, Nowell x1059).

P. 34.

Oriental Building, Manufactures Building, and Cascade Fountain. Courtesy University of Washington Libraries Special Collections (AYP503, UW 28137z).

P. 35.

Seattle schoolchildren. Courtesy University of Washington Libraries Special Collections (AYP527, Nowell x628).

P. 36.

Promotional postcards and pamphlets, left. Courtesy University of Washington Libraries Special Collections (18947, Postcard Collection).

Center. Courtesy University of Washington Libraries Special Collections (N979.7432, Seattle AYPE Pamphlets).

Right. Courtesy Washington State Historical Society (Eph. 979.77718 AL119, 1909).

P. 37.

John Edward Chilberg addresses exposition stockholders. Courtesy University of Washington Libraries Special Collections (AYP185, Nowell x209).

Forestry building under construction. Courtesy University of Washington Libraries Special Collections (AYP516, Nowell x408).

First log of the Arctic Brotherhood Building. Courtesy University of Washington Libraries Special Collections (AYP194, UW 28046).

P. 38.

Hello Bill postcard. Courtesy University of Washington Libraries Special Collections (AYP232, UW 24311).

P. 39.

Skilled plasterers. Courtesy University of Washington Libraries Special Collections (AYP520, Nowell x259).

Model for wolf sculpture. Courtesy Museum of History & Industry (1984.144.1).

P. 40. AND P. 41.

Nome Circle. Courtesy University of Washington Libraries Special Collections (AYP335, Nowell x1812).

P. 42.

1909 University of Washington commencement exercises. Courtesy University of Washington Libraries Special Collections (AYP537, UW 28142z).

Crates of exhibit materials. Courtesy University of Washington Libraries Special Collections (AYP514, UW 27554).

P. 43.

A-Y-P guards and turnstile operators. Courtesy University of Washington Libraries Special Collections (AYP190, Nowell x2833).

P. 44.

Opening Day crowds. Courtesy Washington State Historical Society Asahel Curtis, 12091).

P. 45.

Opening Day pass. Courtesy Museum of History & Industry (1992.1.1).

P. 46.

Daily tickets to the fair. Courtesy Museum of History & Industry (Lib. 1996.13).

P. 47.

Michigan State Society members. Courtesy University of Washington Libraries Special Collections (AYP418, Nowell x2190).

Trolley Trips brochure. Courtesy Dan Keregee.

P. 49.

A-Y-P airship. Courtesy University of Washington Libraries Special Collections (AYP319, PH. Coll. Oakes, AYP 887.1249).

P. 50. AND P. 51.

Court of Honor and Cascade Fountain. Courtesy University of Washington Libraries Special Collections (AYP219, Nowell x1597).

P. 52.

Japanese Rear Admiral Hikojiro Ijichi. Courtesy University of Washington Libraries Special Collections (AYP297, UW 27354z).

P. 53.

Young fairgoers pause near the Geyser Basin. Courtesy University of Washington Libraries Special Collections AYP530, Nowell x1453).

P. 90.

Frank H. Nowell. Courtesy University of Washington Libraries Special Collections (AYP422, Nowell x1144).

Alkali Ike's Wild West and Indian Show. Courtesy University of Washington Libraries Special Collections (AYP606, Nowell x2725).

Gee-string investigators. Courtesy University of Washington Libraries Special Collections (AYP197, UW 27589z).

P. 91.

King Street Station. Courtesy Washington State Historical Society (1943.42.1254).

P. 92.

James J. Hill. Courtesy University of Washington Libraries Special Collections (AYP153, Nowell x3212).

P. 93.

A-Y-P Hostess Association. Courtesy Museum of History & Industry (90.73.127).

P. 94.

Chehalis County booklet. Courtesy Washington State Historical Society (Eph. 979.795 C417c 1909).

P. 95.

Pay Streak tickets. Courtesy University of Washington Libraries Special Collections (T890 D9 A43 1909).

Exposition-themed sheet music. Courtesy Washington State Historical Society (Music 1994.62141).

P. 96.

Dixieland Special Band. Courtesy University of Washington Libraries Special Collections (AYP578, Nowell x1846).

Spanish Theatre. Courtesy University of Washington Libraries Special Collections (AYP623, Nowell x1643).

Alaska Theatre of Sensations. Courtesy University of Washington Libraries Special Collections (AYP605, Nowell x1854).

P. 97.

Temple of Palmistry. Courtesy University of Washington Libraries Special Collections (AYP579, Nowell x2258).

"Don't Marry A Man If He Drinks." Courtesy University of Washington

Libraries Special Collections (Digital Collections, DMM-01, Volume 2).

P. 98.

Ezra Meeker. Courtesy University of Washington Libraries Special Collections (AYP295, PH. Coll. 727).

P. 99.

Good-luck Billikens. Courtesy Museum of History & Industry (Harwood, 1974.5868.184).

Captive balloon. Courtesy Paul Dorpat.

P. 100.

Runners start the mile relay. Courtesy University of Washington Libraries Special Collections (AYP828, Orville J. Rognon PH. Coll. 779.16).

Brass button. Courtesy Dan Kerlee.

P. 101.

French Fete. Courtesy University of Washington Libraries Special Collections (AYP652, UW 28063).

P. 102.

Pay Streak two-step. Courtesy Washington State Historical Society (979.771 C8820 1909).

Columbia Eneutseak. Courtesy Museum of History & Industry (Goetze, 1995.38.37.228).

P. 103.

Pay Streak. Courtesy History Ink.

P. 104.

Performers in Alkali Ike's Wild West Show pose. Courtesy University of Washington Libraries Special Collections (AYP582, Nowell x2188).

P. 105.

Miss Columbia and a ballyhoo spieler. Courtesy University of Washington Libraries Special Collections (C.E. Meldrum AYPE Album, UW 27934z).

P. 106.

A-Y-P Jurors ribbon. Courtesy Museum of History & Industry (1957.1228.6).

P. 107.

Hawaiian officials, hostesses, and musicians. Courtesy University of Washington Libraries Special Collections (AYP405, Nowell x3535).

Conservation Congress pin-back button. Courtesy Dan Kerlee.

P. 108.

Esplanade at the foot of the Pay Streak. Courtesy Museum of History & Industry Nowell, 90.73.155).

P. 109.

Norway Day commemorative ribbon. Courtesy Washington State Historical Society (2004.46.65).

Utah medallion. Courtesy Dan Kerlee.

P. 110.

Official Daily Program. Courtesy University of Washington Libraries Special Collections (T890.D9 A43 1909).

P. 110 AND P. 111.

Dome Circle. Courtesy University of Washington Libraries Special Collections (AYP218, Nowell x1807).

P. 112.

Fairgoers stroll the paths. Courtesy University of Washington Libraries Special Collections AYP266, Nowell x1571).

P. 113.

Felt pennant. Courtesy Museum of History & Industry (1957.1228.6B).

P. 114.

Smith Day contest winners. Courtesy University of Washington Libraries Special Collections (AYP1255, Nowell x3717).

Battle of Gettysburg. Courtesy University of Washington Libraries Special Collections (AYP633, Nowell x2049).

P. 115.

Pin-back button boosting Seattle Day. Courtesy Dan Kerlee.

The "Mayflower" on New England Day. Courtesy Museum of History & Industry (Goetze, 1995.38.37.232).

P. 116.

Seattle Day souvenir ticket. Courtesy History Ink.

South entrance gate. Courtesy University of Washington Libraries Special Collections

P. 117.

A-Y-P 2-cent stamp. Courtesy History Ink.

William Henry Seward statue. Courtesy University of Washington Libraries Special Collections (Seattle Photography Collection, SEA 1945).

P. 118.

Angelo Merlino olive oil diploma. Courtesy Museum of History & Industry (1996.48.1).

P. 119.

China Day participants. Courtesy Museum of History & Industry (Harwood, 1974.5868.174).

P. 120.

Prince Albert the Educated Horse. Courtesy University of Washington Libraries Special Collections (AYP594, Nowell x2958).

Exhibitor's Day ticket. Courtesy Museum of History & Industry (1992.1.2).

Ag-o-nai, a performer in the Igorrote Village. Courtesy University of Washington Libraries Special Collections (AYP892, PH. Coll. 777, Park).

P. 121.

California Building displays. Courtesy University of Washington Libraries Special Collections (AYP045, Nowell x1775).

P. 122.

Livestock show. Courtesy Museum of History & Industry (Goetze, 1995.38.37.200).

Statue of Marcus Whitman. Courtesy Museum of History & Industry (Harwood, 1974.5868.14).

P. 123.

Grand Prize ribbon. Courtesy Museum of History & Industry (1965.3766.2).

President Taft welcome arch. Courtesy Washington State Historical Society (Asahel Curtis, 16414).

P. 125.

President William Howard Taft. Courtesy University of Washington Libraries Special Collections (AYP1232, Nowell x1306).

p. 126.

Crowds of children. Courtesy Museum of History & Industry (Harwood, 1974.5868.141).

Baby Day commemorative ribbon. Courtesy Washington State Historical Society (2004.46.66).

P. 127.

Young Pay Streak performers enjoy an auto tour. Courtesy University of Washington Libraries Special Collections (AYP532, Nowell x1306).

Olympia High School girls. Courtesy University of Washington Libraries Special Collections (AYP298, UW 28138z).

P. 128.

Rainier Beer pin. Courtesy Dan Kerlee.

Assorted A-Y-P pins. Courtesy Dan Kerlee.

Mapleine tray. Courtesy Dan Kerlee.

Two souvenir booklets. Courtesy Dan Kerlee.

China plate. Courtesy Museum of History & Industry (1953.579).

Mineral ore paperweight. Courtesy Dan Kerlee.

Cloisonné pin. Courtesy Dan Kerlee.

A-Y-P logo pin. Courtesy Dan Kerlee.

P. 129.

William Jennings Bryan. Courtesy Washington State Historical Society (14012).

Poster advertising William Jennings Bryan Day. Courtesy Washington State Historical Society (Asahel Curtis, 18814).

P. 130.

European Building illuminated at night. Courtesy University of Washington Libraries Special Collections (AYP139, Nowell x1124).

P. 131.

Ohio Day commemorative ribbon. Courtesy Museum of History & Industry (1984.142.4.17).

Washington State Building was perfect for dancing. Courtesy University of Washington Libraries Special Collections (AYP1204, Nowell x2770).

P. 132.

Pin-back button. Courtesy Museum of History & Industry (1963.3133.32).

P. 132. AND P. 133.

Aerial view from the tethered balloon. Courtesy University of Washington Libraries Special Collections (27926z).

P. 134.

The A-Y-P Auditorium Building was renamed Meany Hall. Courtesy University of Washington Libraries Special Collections (UW Coll. 778.37, UW 2077).

P. 135.

Quilt made from commemorative satin

ribbons. Courtesy Museum of History & Industry (1993.70.1).

P. 136.

The dinner that marked the formal dissolution. Courtesy University of Washington Libraries Special Collections (778.1).

P. 137.

The Burke Museum. Courtesy The Burke Museum.

John Edward Chilberg's silver chalice. Courtesy Museum of History & Industry (1957.1208).

P. 138.

Sunkist used their A-Y-P diploma. Courtesy Dan Kerlee.

P. 139.

Century 21. Courtesy University of Washington Libraries Special Collections (ARC0135, UW Archives).

P. 140.

An aerial view of the University of Washington campus in 1959. Photo by James O. Sneddon, Courtesy University of Washington Special Collections (UW19630z).

P. 141.

Bronze plaque. Courtesy History Ink.

P. 142.

Official map of A-Y-P fairgrounds. Courtesy University of Washington Libraries Special Collections (27945z, Coll. G4284.54:2A4z, 1909.J2).

P. 144.

Administration Building. Courtesy University of Washington Libraries Special Collections (AYP965, PH Coll. 777 PPCC.6502).

Agriculture Building. Courtesy University of Washington Libraries Special Collections (AYP018, Nowell x1636).

P. 145.

Alaska Building. Courtesy University of Washington Libraries Special Collections AYP005, Nowell x1877).

Auditorium Building. Courtesy University of Washington Libraries Special Collections (27906z).

Arctic Brotherhood Building. Courtesy University of Washington Libraries Special Collections (AYP151, Nowell x246).

P. 146.

Canada Building. Courtesy Washington State Historical Society (Goetze, 1995.38.37.48).

California Building. Courtesy University of Washington Libraries Special Collections (AYP040, Nowell x1707).

Chehalis County Building. Courtesy University of Washington Libraries Special Collections (AYP970, Coll. 777, Reid.62).

P. 147.

Education Building. Courtesy University of Washington Libraries Special Collections (AYP542, UW 28091).

Dairy Exhibit Building. Courtesy University of Washington Libraries Special Collections (27913z).

P. 148.

Emergency Hospital. Courtesy Daryl McClary.

Fine Arts Building. Courtesy Washington State Historical Society (1994.80.7, AYPE, Nowell).

European/Foreign Building. Courtesy University of Washington Libraries Special Collections (AYP091, Nowell x1315).

P. 149.

Forestry Building. Courtesy University of Washington Libraries Special Collections (27907z).

Fire Station. Courtesy University of Washington Libraries Special Collections (AYP092, Nowell x1356).

P. 150.

Hawaii Building. Courtesy University of Washington Libraries Special Collections (AYP088, Nowell x2848).

Good Roads Building. Courtesy University of Washington Libraries Special Collections (727.391, UW 13719).

P. 151.

Hoo-Hoo House. Courtesy University of Washington Libraries Special Collections (27922z).

Idaho Building. Courtesy University of Washington Libraries Special Collections (AYP068, Nowell x2180).

Japan Building. Courtesy University of Washington Libraries Special Collections (AYP062, Nowell x2820).

P. 152.

Life Saving Station. Courtesy Washington State Historical Society (1994.80.9 AYPE, Nowell).

King County Building. Courtesy University of Washington Libraries Special Collections (27927z).

Machinery Building. Courtesy Washington State Historical Society (1994.80.21 AYP).

P. 153.

Michigan Club Building. Courtesy University of Washington Libraries Special Collections (27917z).

Manufactures Building. Courtesy University of Washington Libraries Special Collections (AYP271, Nowell x 1538).

P. 154.

New York Building. Courtesy University of Washington Libraries Special Collections (AYP082, Nowell x1809).

Mines Building. Courtesy University of Washington Libraries Special Collections (27921z).

P. 155.

Oriental Building. Courtesy University of Washington Libraries Special Collections (AYP165, Nowell x888).

Philippine Building. Courtesy University of Washington Libraries Special Collections (AYP080, Nowell x1576).

Oregon Building. Courtesy University of Washington Libraries Special Collections (AYP104, Nowell x1545).

P. 156.

Power House. Courtesy University of Washington Libraries Special Collections (AYP1165, UW20276z).

Spokane County Building. Courtesy University of Washington Libraries Special Collections (AYP084, Nowell x1986).

P. 157.

Swedish Building. Courtesy University of Washington Libraries Special Collections (27212z).

United States Government Building. Courtesy University of Washington Libraries Special Collections (ARC 0014, U.W. Architects, Accession No. 73-28, Box 10).

P. 158.

Utah Building. Courtesy Museum of History & Industry (90.73.87).

Washington State Building. Courtesy University of Washington Libraries Special Collections (AYP449, PH Coll.727.606).

P. 159.

Yakima County Building. Courtesy University of Washington Libraries Special Collections (AYP079, Nowell x1503).

Washington Woman's Building. Courtesy University of Washington Libraries Special Collections (2792z, PH Coll. 777, AYPE Postcard Collection).

P. 160.

John C. Olmsted's axial plan. Courtesy National Park Service, Frederick Law Olmsted National Historic Site and Friends of Seattle's Olmsted Parks, hand colored ca. March 1909.

Fairgoers enjoyed strolling. Courtesy University of Washington Libraries Special Collections (AYP324260, Neg. Nowell x2282).

The Cascades under construction. Courtesy University of Washington Libraries Special Collections (AYP324, Neg. UW 11727).

P. 161.

Olmsted designed a rustic trestle bridge. Courtesy University of Washington Libraries Special Collections (AYP264, Neg. UW 28050).

Pathways along Lake Washington. Courtesy University of Washington Libraries Special Collections (AYP1221, Neg. Nowell x2781).

Fairgoers enjoyed. Courtesy University of Washington Libraries Special Collections (AYP472, Neg. Nowell x1999).

A graceful swath. Courtesy University of Washington Libraries Special Collections (AYP189, Neg. Nowell x2388).

P. 162.

A-Y-P coupon tickets. Courtesy University of Washington Libraries Special Collections (AYP141, Nowell x1275).

P. 163.

Gold seekers as Chilkoot Pass, Alaska. Courtesy University of Washington Libraries Special Collections (LAR230, LaRoche 2132).

Hotel Savoy brochure. Courtesy Washington State Historical Society (Eph 979.77718/Se18 1909).

Luggage tag. Courtesy Dan Kerlee.

Seattle brochure. Courtesy HistoryInk.

P. 164.

Grading crew level site for Pay Streak. Courtesy University of Washington Libraries Special Collections (AYP523, Nowell x349).

Division of Works uniform button. Courtesy Dan Kerlee.

Forestry Building floor plan. Courtesy University of Washington Libraries Special Collections (ARC 0005, UW Architects, Accession #73-28, Box 2).

A. W. Lewis. Courtesy University of Washington Libraries Special Collections (AYP460, UW 28047).

P. 165.

Marion Hay. Courtesy University of Washington Libraries Special Collections (AYP523, Nowell x349).

Flags of the International Union of the American Republics. Courtesy University of Washington Libraries Special Collections (AYP255, Postcard Collection).

First Olmsted Brothers' A-Y-P plan. Courtesy University of Washington Libraries Special Collections (N979.7432, Seattle AYPE Pamphlets).

Ferris Wheel. Courtesy University of Washington Libraries Special Collections (AYP595, Nowell x2801).

Seattle Chamber of Commerce brochure. Courtesy University of Washington Libraries Special Collections (N979.7432, Seattle AYPE Pamphlets, Folder 2).

P. 166.

Invitation. Courtesy University of Washington Libraries Special Collections (AYPE Memorabilia Collection 1/6, #296-3v256b).

Olympia High School demonstrators. Courtesy University of Washington Libraries Special Collections (AYP659, Nowell x2955).

Aso and Soya. Courtesy Washington State Historical Society (2007.01.121).

Vancouver, B.C., Daily World headquarters. Courtesy University of Washington Libraries Special Collections (AYP456, Nowell x3875).

Spoon. Courtesy University of Washington Libraries Special Collections (AYPE Memorabilia Collection, 979.7432).

P. 167.

King County brochure. Courtesy University of Washington Libraries Special Collections (N979.743z, Seattle AYPE Pamphlets, Folder 2).

Spokane pin-back button. Courtesy Dan Kerlee.

Giant wooden dice. Courtesy University of Washington Libraries Special Collections (AYP313, PH Coll. 78).

Woman Suffrage Day ribbon. Courtesy Washington State Historical Society (Ephemera c208.0.30).

P. 168.

Snohomish County Day ribbon. Courtesy Museum of History & Industry (1963.2921.1).

Shelton booster button. Courtesy Museum of History & Industry (1963.2921.11).

Music pavilion at night. Courtesy University of Washington Libraries Special Collections (AYP114, Nowell x947).

A-Y-P season pass. Courtesy Museum of History & Industry (1992.1.3).

Historical Exhibit Director badge. Courtesy Washington State Historical Society (1916.56.1).

P. 169.

Model of Mormon Tabernacle. Courtesy University of Washington Libraries Special Collections (AYP126, Nowell x1948).

Japan Day ribbon. Courtesy Washington State Historical Society (1999.20.1).

Arrival Arch. Courtesy HistoryInk.

Smith Day ribbon. Courtesy University of Washington Libraries Special Collections (AYPE #296-3 V256b, Memorabilia 1/6).

Vacuum Tube Railway. Courtesy University of Washington Libraries Special Collections (AYP588, Nowell x2221).

P. 170.

Idaho Day ribbon. Courtesy Museum of History & Industry (1960.18185).

San Diego Day ribbon. Courtesy Museum of History & Industry (1963.3133.10).

Stevens County Day ribbon. Courtesy Washington State Historical Society (2004.46.174).

Guess-Your-Weight concession. Courtesy University of Washington Libraries Special Collections (AYP589, Nowell x2724).

Carnation Milk advertising postcard. Courtesy University of Washington Libraries Special Collections (23379z).

P. 171.

Shooting Gallery. Courtesy University of Washington Libraries Special Collections (AYP590, Nowell x2230).

A-Y-P playing cards. Courtesy Washington State Historical Society (2003.170.1).

Cover of Washington State Commission final report. Courtesy Washington State Historical Society (EPH 979.77718/R299al 1910).

U. S. Government Building Souvenir pin. Courtesy University of Washington Libraries Special Collections (979.7432, AYPE).

P. 172.

Frank Nowell's team of photographers. Courtesy University of Washington Libraries Special Collections (AYP077, Neg. Nowell x2860).

FRONT ENDPAPERS.

Birds Eye View. Courtesy University of Washington Libraries Special Collections (AYP462, Neg. 1378).

BACK ENDPAPERS.

Colorful postcards. Courtesy Daryl McClary.

BACK COVER.

The rustic benches. Courtesy University of Washington Libraries Special Collections (AYP034, Neg. Nowell x1965).

AFTERWORD

THE WASHINGTON GOVERNOR'S MANSION ALSO celebrated its centennial in 2009, in concert with the A-Y-P. On hand for the official observation were Governor Christine Gregoire and her husband, Mike, at left; former Governor Daniel J. Evans and his wife, Nancy, center; and former Secretary of State Ralph Monroe, right. It is thought that the mansion was constructed in part to host dignitaries visiting the A-Y-P. Just as the fair provided a platform for promoting woman suffrage, so, too, did the new Governor's Mansion. At the mansion housewarming in January 1909, suffragists wearing their finest gowns and brightest jewels lobbied the legislative committee chairman who was holding their suffrage bill hostage and successfully changed his mind. On November 8, 1910, Washington became the fifth state to grant women the vote, a full decade before an amendment to the U. S. Constitution gave women the vote nationwide.

ACKNOWLEDGMENTS

HIGHEST THANKS TO JENNIFER OTT, ON WHOSE THOROUGH RESEARCH skills and insightful opinions we have relied. A-Y-P collector Dan Kerlee generously shared his voluminous knowledge of the fair and his impressive artifact collection. Paul Dorpat's decades of accumulated thought on the A-Y-P were extremely helpful. Dan Kerege, XNGH, Doc Maynard Chapter 54-40, E Clampus Vitus, gave access to his A-Y-P materials and served as artifact spotter. Dr. Reimert Ravenholt shined light on health issues at the fair, particularly water quality. Jane Powell Thomas shared with us the personal archives of her grandfather, UW regent John H. Powell. Daryl McClary gave us access to his A-Y-P postcard collection and other materials. Amy Dunn Caldwell, ARNP at Seattle Children's hospital, helped research the history of baby incubators in Washington. Jerome Arbes and Anne Knight of the Friends of Seattle's Olmsted Parks shared their knowledge and historical materials. Carol Van Natta at the University of Washington, Tacoma, shared her memories and research of the A-Y-P's 75th anniversary. Thanks also to the Washington Women's History Consortium and to its director, Shanna Stevenson. A generous grant from the consortium funded HistoryLink.org essays documenting woman suffrage activities in Washington during the A-Y-P Exposition, and these essays greatly aided our coverage of these events in this volume.

Many people provided great assistance in the historical archives where we did our digging. Among them special thanks goes to Carla Rickerson, Nicolette Bromberg, Gary Lundell, Kris Kinsey, and others at the University of Washington Libraries Special Collections; the staff of the Microforms Department at University of Washington; Shauna Gandy, Scott Daniels, and volunteers of the Oregon Historical Society Research Library; Anne Frantilla at Seattle Municipal Archives; Jodee Fenton at the Seattle Public Library; David Nicandri, Joy Werlink, Elaine Miller, and Nancy Jackson at the Washington State Historical Society; Carolyn Marr, Kristen Halunen, and Howard Giske at the Museum of History & Industry; Alan Barnett at Utah State Archives; and Greg Lange at Washington State Archives, Puget Sound Region.

Paula Becker thanks Barry, Hunter, Sawyer, and Lillie Brown for their patience, encouragement, and support, and David and Shirleen Becker for their repeated assistance.

Alan Stein thanks Doc Maynard Chapter 54-40, E Clampus Vitus, whose understanding and ongoing support of HistoryLink.org have been sustaining.

End Elevation Agriculture Building, Alaska-Yukon-Pacific Exposition, Seattle, Wash. 1909.